The Ultimate Teen Girl's Survival Guide

Jessica Blakely

CONTENTS

INTRODUCTION

"Beep! Beep! Beep!" My alarm clock blares, jolting me awake. Another day, another whirlwind of teenage chaos awaits. Welcome to my life, where the pressure never seems to let up. I'm Emily, a 15-year-old girl trying to navigate the treacherous waters of adolescence. Let me tell you, it's no walk in the park. I like to journal and keep track of my journey to trace my progress and what I need to work on.

First things first, my body decides to throw me a curveball. As if dealing with school, extracurriculars, and the ever-demanding social scene isn't enough, I wake up to the unwelcome arrival of my period. Great timing, right? My tummy churns with discomfort, but there's no time to dwell on it. Life waits for no one.

Today's agenda is jam-packed with challenges that would make even the most organized adult break into a cold sweat. I have a math test first period, and let's just say numbers and I have a complicated relationship. Then, there's an English class speech presentation looming over me like a dark cloud. Public speaking? Yeah, not exactly my forte. Especially with the "mean girls" watching my every move in English class, all because Harry Stone decided to make me his stalker focus this semester, and the queen bee of the mean girls squad is hung up on him. Gross, as if!

But wait, there's more! A new chemistry research project awaits, and guess who my lab partner is? Ethan—the new and undeniably handsome boy who recently joined our school. Talk about adding a dash of nerves to the mix. Will we make a great team or will it be a recipe for disaster? Only time will tell.

As if my academic hurdles weren't enough, I also have a swim meet later today. The coach is eyeing me for the junior team's state championship gala event. No pressure, right? I'm the favorite, but that doesn't mean I can afford to let my guard down. Every stroke, every kick, every breath counts.

In the midst of this whirlwind, there's one person I can always turn to: Aunt Moira. She's my confidante, my rock, and the one who truly understands what it's like to be a teenage girl in this crazy world. With my parents caught up in their own lives, Aunt Moira is the one who listens, advises, and helps me navigate the ups and downs of adolescence. I bet I will be texting her a lot today. Or if she is busy during the day, we might have one of our epic video calls tonight.

"Mom says you're late!" screeches Hannah, the annoying 2.0 version of me. She's 12 years old, and we share a love-hate relationship. Okay, maybe she worships me a bit, but it can get exhausting on the bedazzled pedestal of your younger sibling.

I guess I'd better seize the day...after I've changed the sheets, of course.

I know I sound like a hot mess, but I'd like to think of myself as a level-headed teen who is merely an adult under construction. Does that make sense? I usually prefer to work on myself by myself by doing research and cross-referencing data I acquire with what's really going on in the lives of my peeps. As a last resort, I lean on Aunt Moira and of course, my journal.

Like all level-headed girls my age, I get put to the test in every sphere of life, and I know that each challenge is a chance to level up. Kinda like a video game in which I am the hero who has to pass through all the stages of teenagehood in order to finish the game with a decent high score.

In this game called "Emily Runs the Gauntlet," I imagine I've started out as a caterpillar, and I am soaking up all the knowledge and experiences I can so that when it happens, I will emerge into the world as a butterfly. Yeah, I know; I have some kinda crazy imagination, right? But if you are also a caterpillar gal looking to connect as you go through your own transformation, you are more than welcome to share in the fun of the juggling act that is the journey of my life.

In fact, buckle up and join me on this rollercoaster ride through the teenage years. Together, we'll face the challenges, celebrate the victories, and discover what it truly means to survive and thrive in this wild journey called life. Let's dive in, shall we?

Chapter 1

THE MIND GYM

Have you ever wondered how hard our teen brains are working these days? It's like they're running a never-ending thought marathon. From the moment we wake up to the time we hit the hay, our minds are constantly buzzing.

But here's the kicker: Research shows we have more than 6,000 thoughts a day (Raypole, 2022)! Yep, it's like an overdrive mode for our brains. They measured this during a study using brain scans while people watched movies. Each new thought transitioned about 6.5 times per minute (Raypole, 2022).

Now, not all thoughts are sunshine and rainbows. Some are downright pesky and stick around like unwanted guests, messing with our moods. Negative thoughts? They're the culprits. They can pile up, especially if we're dealing with anxiety or depression. It's like a thought tornado in our heads.

But don't sweat it. Your personality plays a role in your thought factory. Super chill minds are quieter, but if you lean toward the neurotic side, brace for a thought avalanche.

Now, let's talk about intrusive thoughts. They're like pop-up ads in your head, but not the fun kind. Most people get 'em occasionally, but if they're camping out in your mind, it might be time to chat with a mental health pro.

So, where do these thoughts even come from? It's like your brain's cells are sending each other secret messages. But don't worry, you don't have to be a thought slave. We'll learn how to ride the thought waves like pros in this chapter.

Stress and Anxiety

I'm here to spill the tea on the rollercoaster ride of teen stress and anxiety. But don't worry, this isn't your typical "adults-know-best" spiel. Nope, we're diving right into the teen zone (Raising Children Network, 2017). So, grab your favorite snacks, and let's dish about the madness that is our teenage years.

Stress, Stress, and More Stress

Okay, so stress is like that annoying pop-up ad that keeps showing up on your favorite game. It's always lurking around, and you can't seem to escape it. It hits you when your math homework suddenly looks like hieroglyphics or when your crush finally texts you back (cue the heart palpitations).

The Dreaded "A" Word – Anxiety

Anxiety is basically like having a gremlin living in your brain. It makes you worry about stuff that hasn't even happened yet, like a surprise pop quiz or whether your Instagram post got enough likes. Oh, and it comes with all those lovely side effects—the shaky hands, the racing heart, and my personal favorite, the butterflies in the stomach. Sometimes, it feels like a circus in there!

Teenage Brain Versus Chaos

Picture this: Your brain is like a mad scientist's lab. It's frantically mixing emotions, hormones, and the sudden urge to dye your hair neon green. Yeah, that's adolescence for you. Our brains are changing faster than the latest TikTok trends, and it's completely normal to feel like you're on a never-ending emotional rollercoaster.

School Drama and Social Shenanigans

Starting high school? Joining a new club? These things are just code for "potential social landmines." You worry about fitting in, making friends, or not tripping in the cafeteria. But guess what? Everyone else is just as nervous as you are. So, embrace your quirks and remember that being yourself is the ultimate superpower.

Adulting 101 – Responsibility and Stuff

As we get older, the responsibilities start piling up like laundry that never ends. Money, jobs, chores—they all become a thing. It's okay to feel anxious about these adult-ish tasks. Take it one step at a time, and don't be afraid to ask for help. Even superheroes have sidekicks, right?

Coping With the Crazy

So, how do we tackle these teen troubles? Communication is key. Talk to someone you trust about what's going on inside that wild brain of yours. Whether it's your BFF, your mom, or even a counselor, sharing your feelings can be super liberating.

Embrace Your Inner Daredevil

Here's a secret: Feeling a little anxious can sometimes be a good thing. It's like your brain's way of prepping you for exciting adventures, like public speaking or crushing that big exam. So, don't shy away from challenges—embrace them with the confidence of a pro gamer.

The Power of Self-Talk

Positive self-talk is your secret weapon against anxiety. Tell yourself you can handle it, even when your inner gremlin says otherwise. Be your own biggest cheerleader because you've got this!

Being the Best Role Model (or at Least Trying)

Guess what? Even our parents dealt with their share of teen drama. They can actually be pretty cool allies. Ask them about their wild teenage stories, and you'll see they weren't always the boring adults they are now. Plus, you might learn a few tricks for surviving your own teenage tornado.

Teen Toolbox for Chillaxing

Need some tools to keep your cool? Try out stuff like going for a walk, doing breathing exercises, or even zoning out to your favorite music. It's like self-care but for teens.

When to Call in the Pros

If your stress and anxiety are reaching superhero levels of intensity and sticking around like your annoying little sibling, it might be time to call in the pros. Talk to your school counselor or a therapist—they're basically the Avengers of mental health.

So there you have it, my fellow teens. Life as a teenager is like a crazy, unpredictable game, and stress and anxiety are just some of the levels we have to beat. But remember, you're not alone, and you're stronger than you think. Let's face these challenges together and come out as the champions we were born to be!

Mindfulness

So, during one of my cozy catch-ups with Aunt Moira, I told her about this girl in my class who appeared to have anxiety issues. Carmen was a very focused student in her freshman year. Even though we were never particularly close, I believe she could use someone to talk to because she is quite withdrawn and introverted.

Then Aunt Moira told me about how practicing mindfulness can help with stress and just being mentally present more. I know it might sound like some zen stuff, but trust me, it's a total game-changer for us teens dealing with stress and anxiety. So, grab your favorite cozy blanket, and let me tell you all about what Aunt Moira and I chatted about regarding why practicing mindfulness is a must—at home, school, and with friends.

So, what's this mindfulness thing, anyway? In a nutshell, it's like hitting the pause button on your racing thoughts and just being in the moment.

It's about noticing your thoughts and feelings without getting all caught up in them (Spring, 2023). Paying close attention to the world around you without judgment is the first step toward becoming more mindful. It's kinda like being the chill observer of your own mind without trying to change anything. And here's the deal—it can totally help with stress and anxiety.

Benefits of Mindfulness

Now, why should you care about mindfulness? Well, let me break it down for you:

- **Self-regulation:** Mindfulness gives you the power to control your emotions (Spring, 2023). It's like having a secret weapon to handle those intense feelings that come with being a teenager. You'll learn to be besties with your emotions, leading to better emotional well-being.

- **Emotional awareness:** You'll become a feelings detective, spotting and understanding your emotions like a pro (Spring, 2023). This can boost your emotional well-being and help you navigate the teenage rollercoaster.

- **Say bye to negative thoughts:** Mindfulness helps you kick those nasty, unhelpful thoughts to the curb (Spring, 2023). You'll start dealing with them like a boss, using that mindful perspective to stay calm and collected.

Hacks to Finding Your Zen

Ready to give mindfulness a shot? There are loads of cool techniques you can try (Spring, 2023).

- **Meditation:** Yep, it's not just for yogis. Meditation helps train your attention and tame your emotions. Find a style that suits you, and start practicing. You can find loads of guided meditations online to enhance your mindfulness. Some of these sessions are body scan meditations, mindful breathing, mindful eating, loving-kindness meditation, mindful movement, and mindful thinking (Vo, n.d.).

- **Body scan:** This practice involves scanning your body to become aware of sensations like pain, tension, numbness, and relaxation. It can improve sleep, reduce pain, and alleviate stress and anxiety. Check out the cool body scan activity at the end of this chapter.

- **Yoga or stretching routine:** Incorporate a short yoga or stretching routine into your day. Feel every move and notice what's happening in your body.

- **Mindful breathing:** Whenever, wherever, you can focus on your breath to bring you back to the now and calm your thoughts. When you breathe deeply and slowly, it sends a message to your body that everything is A-OK. It can lower your stress and help you feel more in control. Check out the cool breathing activity at the end of this chapter.

- **Grounding techniques:** Stand or sit with your feet flat on the ground, feeling the connection to the earth. Notice the sensations in your body.

- **Walk and be mindful:** Take a stroll while practicing mindfulness. Feel your feet lifting and landing, the air against your skin, and the sounds of your surroundings.

- **Connect with nature:** Ditch the screens for a bit. Nature is calling! Head outside and soak in the natural goodness around you.

- **Mindful eating:** Pay attention to the flavors, textures, and smells of your food. Eat slowly, savoring each bite. Doing this also helps you really enjoy every bite!

- **Gratitude diary:** Jot down three cool things each day. It's like capturing good vibes and turning them into a daily mood booster.

- **Journaling:** Pour your thoughts onto paper. It's like therapy but without the awkward silence. Check out the cool journaling activity at the end of chapter 6.

Practice Makes Perfect

Integrating mindfulness into your life might take some time. But that's totally okay! Here are some tips to help you out (Spring, 2023):

- Be patient with yourself. Rome wasn't built in a day, and neither is your mindfulness practice.

- Experiment with different techniques. Find what vibes with you.

- Create a cozy, distraction-free space for your practice. Bye-bye, phone!

So, there you have it; stress and anxiety doesn't have to run the show. Mindfulness is our secret weapon for a more relaxed life. It's like a superhero cape for the mind. With some practice, we'll notice a real difference in how we feel. So, go ahead, embrace mindfulness, and let's conquer the teenage world, one mindful breath at a time!

Mental Health

Mental health covers your psychological, social, and emotional well-being. It's like a superhero shield that helps you develop, form strong relationships, adapt to changes, and tackle life's curveballs (Raising Children Network, 2019).

As you go through the exciting journey of becoming a teenager, you might face some twists and turns. Your mental health plays a starring role in your happiness, your relationships with family and friends, and how you handle life's ups and downs. It's a big deal!

The Perks of Good Mental Health

When your mental health is in tip-top shape, amazing things happen (Raising Children Network, 2019):

- You feel happier and more positive and enjoy life to the fullest.

- You can bounce back from tough times and setbacks.

- Building strong relationships with family and friends becomes a breeze.

- Staying active and eating healthily becomes a natural choice.

- Getting involved in activities you love brings a sense of accomplishment.

- Quality sleep becomes your superpower.

- You feel like you belong to your community, making you part of something bigger.

Being a teenager means going through heaps of changes, both inside and out. Your brain is still developing, and you're dealing with all sorts of challenges. But guess what? We're here to help you make sense of it all!

How to Boost Teenage Mental Health

Here are some fantastic tips to keep your mental health in tip-top shape (Raising Children Network, 2019):

- **Share the love:** Show your affection and care in ways that make you feel comfy, whether it's through hugs, smiles, or just hanging out together.

- **Stay connected:** Let your family and friends know you're interested in their lives. Celebrate their achievements, big or small, and value their thoughts and opinions.

- **Quality time:** Spend one-on-one and family time with loved ones. These moments create precious memories.

- **Talk it out:** If you're feeling down or facing challenges, open up. Talking about what's bothering you can make a world of difference. Remember, you're never alone.

- **Seek help:** If you ever need guidance or someone to talk to, reach out to trusted family members, friends, teachers, or a health professional. They're there to support you.

- **Physical health:** Take care of your physical health. Exercise, eat well, and get enough sleep to boost your mood and energy levels.

A Note on Alcohol and Drugs

Steering clear of alcohol and drugs is essential for your mental health. These substances can be risky and lead to problems. These include performance and attention-enhancing drugs that can lead to addiction.

Recognizing Signs That You Might Need Help

Sometimes, we all have off days. But if you notice any of the following signs for more than a few weeks, it's essential to talk to someone (Raising Children Network, 2019):

- feeling sad often or having a drop in school performance.

- constant worries or fears.

- unexplained physical symptoms like aches or loss of appetite.

- struggling to fit in at school or with friends.

- out-of-character behaviors like aggression, anger, or destructive actions.

- sleep problems, nightmares, or other disruptions.

How to Talk About Mental Health

If you're worried about your mental health or a friend's, starting a conversation is a powerful step (Raising Children Network, 2019):

- Remind yourself that even adults sometimes need help.

- Acknowledge that it's common to feel worried, stressed, or sad.

- Encourage open conversations to put things in perspective and seek different viewpoints.

- Suggest other trustworthy people your friend can talk to, like family members, friends, or professionals.

- Emphasize that seeking professional help is confidential.

Getting Help for Teenage Mental Health

Remember, you don't have to face mental health challenges alone. Seek professional help as early as possible because mental health problems do get better with treatment. Reach out to (Raising Children Network, 2019)

- your GP (general practitioner or family doctor)

- school counselors

- psychologists and counselors

- social workers

- community health centers

- local or state/territory mental health services

- and, of course, your parents!

Taking care of your mental health is essential, and it's okay to ask for help when you need it. You've got this, and there's a whole world of support waiting to help you shine bright!

Stay awesome, and take care of your mental health!

Coping With Grief

Grief can be a whirlwind of feelings, such as sadness, anger, confusion, and even guilt. Understand that it's entirely normal to experience these emotions. Give yourself permission to feel and process them. Remember, it's okay not to be okay sometimes.

- **Open up:** Sharing your thoughts and emotions is a powerful way to navigate grief. Find someone you trust, whether it's a close friend, a family member, or a counselor, and confide in them. They can provide comfort, lend a sympathetic ear, and offer support during this challenging time. You don't have to carry the weight of your grief alone.

- **Create a safe space:** Establish a personal sanctuary where you can retreat when grief feels overwhelming. This space can be a cozy corner in your room filled with comforting items or a private journal where you can pour out your thoughts and feelings. Having a designated safe space allows you to process your emotions without judgment.

- **Self-care matters:** Engaging in self-care activities is crucial when you're grieving. These activities can be anything that brings you comfort and peace, whether it's reading a favorite book, creating art, going for a walk, or practicing relaxation techniques. Taking time for yourself and focusing on self-care can help alleviate some of the emotional burdens that come with grief.

- **Support groups:** Seek out support groups specifically designed for teens dealing with grief. Connecting with others who are going through similar experiences can provide a sense of belonging and understanding. Sharing your grief journey with people who can relate can be profoundly comforting, and you may gain insights and coping strategies from their experiences.

- **Memorialize and remember:** Honoring the memory of your loved one can be a beautiful and healing way to cope with grief. Consider creating rituals, memorials, or personal keepsakes that remind you of the special moments you shared. Planting a tree, making a scrapbook, or writing letters to your loved one are meaningful ways to keep their memory alive in your heart.

- **Time is a healer:** Grief doesn't adhere to a fixed timeline, and there's no "right" way to grieve. Healing takes time, and it's a unique journey for each person. Be patient with yourself as you move through the grieving process. There's no rush to "get over it." Your emotions and healing will progress at your own pace, and that's perfectly okay.

- **Professional help:** If grief becomes overwhelming and feels insurmountable, don't hesitate to seek professional help from a therapist or counselor. These professionals are trained to guide you through the complex emotions of grief and provide you with coping strategies tailored to your needs. Seeking assistance from a mental health expert can be a vital step in your healing journey. Remember, reaching out for help is a sign of strength, not weakness.

Activity 1: 4-7-8 Breathing Exercise

Here is a great way to improve mindfulness with the most basic activity of all—breathing!

4-7-8 Breathing is a cool, simple way to relax and take charge of your feelings. It's all about breathing in, holding, and then breathing out. Here's how to do it (Fletcher, 2019):

1. Get comfy. Find a cozy spot to sit or lie down.

2. Gently touch your tongue to the tissue just behind your top front teeth.

3. Empty your lungs by breathing out completely.

4. Breathe in slowly through your nose for a count of 4 seconds.

5. Hold your breath for 7 seconds.

6. Breathe out strong through your mouth, making a "whoosh" sound for 8 seconds.

7. Repeat this cycle up to 4 times.

4-7-8 Breathing is like a way to power up your mind. It's a simple way to calm down, sleep better, and be more chill. Give it a try and see how it makes you feel!

If you want a little help, there are awesome apps that can remind you to breathe and even time your breaths for you. You can find them in app stores like Apple or Google Play.

Activity 2: Body Scan Exercise

Before we begin, make sure you're sitting comfortably. It's like finding the perfect position that feels right for you—not too stiff and not too slouchy. If you like, close your eyes, or if you prefer to keep them open, gently gaze at the floor (*5-Minute Mindfulness Body Scan Script for Teens*, n.d.).

1. Take a moment to pay attention to your breath. Feel the air enter-

ing and leaving your body. Breathe naturally; no need to change anything.

2. Now, focus on your in-breath. Feel the entire journey of the breath as it flows in. It's like taking in the full story of your in-breath. And then, follow your out-breath, from beginning to end.

3. As you keep your awareness on your breathing, bring your attention up to your forehead. Notice any sensations there. You might feel the energy of your thoughts behind your eyes and at your temples. Relax your facial muscles. Imagine the tension melting away. Shift your attention to your mouth, sensing the emptiness of that space. Be aware of your neck and throat, and let go of any tightness there. As you send your breath down into your body, allow your awareness to follow.

4. Slowly glide your focus across your shoulders, gently releasing any tension you might feel. Keep moving your attention down through your biceps, your elbows, forearms, and wrists. Notice your hands; feel the sensations in all ten fingers.

5. If your mind starts to wander, no worries! Just pause and gently guide your attention back to your breathing. Do this with kindness toward yourself. If it's tough, you can use a simple phrase like, "May I be at ease."

6. Now, bring your awareness back to the center of your body, focusing on the sensations of your breath at your belly. Allow your belly to soften as you feel the rise and fall with each breath.

7. Feel the pull of gravity, drawing your attention deeper into your body. Notice the weight of your body resting in your chair and the points where it touches. This is your body, seated, breathing.

8. Extend your awareness to the tops of your thighs and move down to your knees. Continue down your legs, feeling the front shin bones and the calf muscles at the back. Finally, arrive at your feet resting on the floor. Pay full attention first to your left foot, then gently shift your focus to your right foot, both feet firmly grounded.

9. Now, broaden your awareness to encompass your entire body. Recognize that there's a body here, sitting and breathing. Let your awareness settle into your whole body.

10. Whenever you notice your mind wandering away from the present moment, simply return it to the breath and the sensations in your body.

You've just completed a one-minute body scan! It's a quick way to check in with yourself and find a moment of calm in your day.

Chapter 2

NETIQUETTE AND ONLINE SAFETY

Amelia and I are BFFs, sharing everything. But one day, she called, crying about cyberbullying. Our fun online world turned into a nightmare. I felt helpless, but I knew I had to understand the digital game. So, I started learning, reading articles, watching docs, and asking tech-savvy friends. That's when I found "netiquette" – the guide to online manners and safety. Amelia's pain inspired me to create a teen-friendly netiquette guide to empower others. Let's conquer the digital jungle together and become savvy and kind digital legends!

The Impact of Social Media on Self-Esteem

"Okay, so here's the deal: Social media is more than just scrolling through memes and chatting with friends. It's time to dive into the real stuff and talk about how social media actually affects us, for better or worse.

FOMO – The Fear of Missing Out

Ever heard of FOMO? It's that annoying feeling that everyone else is out there having the time of their lives while you're stuck at home. And guess what? Social media can make it even worse (Ehmke, 2023). You see your friends posting about epic parties, dreamy vacations, or just hanging out with their squad, and suddenly, your cozy night on the couch with Netflix doesn't seem so cool anymore.

The Comparison Game – Am I Good Enough?

We all want to fit in and be liked, right? But when you're constantly comparing your life to those perfectly edited Instagram feeds, it can seriously mess with your self-esteem. Here's the thing Social media doesn't always show the real story. People often post their highlight reels, not the behind-the-scenes struggles (Ehmke, 2023). So, don't be too hard on yourself.

Cyberbullying – A Real and Scary Thing

Unfortunately, some of us have had to deal with online bullies. They hide behind screens and say hurtful things they would never dare to say in person. It's crucial to stand up against cyberbullying and report it (Ehmke, 2023). Nobody deserves to be treated that way, and we need to have each other's backs.

The Imposter Syndrome – Who Am I, Really?

Sometimes, we create an online persona that's not quite like our true selves. Trying to be someone we're not can lead to feeling like a total fake. But here's the truth it's okay to be YOU (Ehmke, 2023). Authenticity is what rocks, and you don't need to pretend to be someone else to be awesome.

Anxiety – The Constant Connection

We're always connected, and let's be real, it can get overwhelming. It feels like we need to respond to texts and notifications ASAP. But here's a reminder: it's important to take breaks and unplug. Your mental health matters more than that next like or comment (Ehmke, 2023). So, give yourself permission to disconnect and recharge.

Communication Skills – Are We Losing Them?

Texting is cool and all, but we shouldn't forget how to have face-to-face conversations. Non-verbal cues, body language, and eye contact – they're all part of effective communication. Let's not let screens replace real connections (Ehmke, 2023). So, put down your phone once in a while and have a good old-fashioned chat with someone.

Real Friendships Versus Virtual Ones

Online friends are great, no doubt about it. But let's not forget the magic of sharing laughter and making memories in person. Don't let your screen time steal away those real-life moments (Ehmke, 2023). So, make sure to nurture your offline friendships, too. They're the ones that truly count.

Trust Your Parents (Sometimes)

Believe it or not, your parents might actually be onto something when they ask you to put down your phone during dinner or limit your screen time. They've been through this tech stuff, too, and know the importance of finding balance (Ehmke, 2023). So, maybe it's worth listening to them once in a while.

So, what's the bottom line? Social media can be a lot of fun, but it's crucial to be aware of its impact. Stay true to yourself, keep an eye out for cyberbullying, and remember that life beyond the screen is where the real adventures happen. It's all about finding that balance, my friends!

How to Tackle Cyberbullying Like a Pro

Amelia and I came up with a plan to tackle her cyberbullying problem. It's not easy, but we've got the tools to stand strong against it. Here's what we came up with together:

- **Block the bullies:** First things first: block those bullies. If someone's making you uncomfortable or being mean online, don't hesitate to hit that block button (Patchin, 2017). It worked for me, and it can work for you, too. Remember, you're in control of your online space.

- **Ignore the hate:** Sometimes, bullies are just looking for a reaction. By ignoring their hurtful comments or messages, you take away their power (Patchin, 2017). It's like denying them the attention they crave. Trust me, it can be pretty effective!

- **Get your parents involved:** Your parents are there to support you. If you're facing cyberbullying, don't hesitate to open up to them. You're not alone in this battle. They can offer advice and comfort and even help you report the bully if needed (Patchin, 2017). Communication with your parents is crucial.

- **Tech break:** If the cyberbullying is getting to be too much, consider taking a break from technology. Log off for a while and give yourself a breather (Patchin, 2017). It's essential to protect your mental health above all else.

- **Report the behavior:** Most online platforms have reporting systems for abusive behavior. Don't hesitate to use them. By reporting the bully, you not only protect yourself but potentially others too (Patchin, 2017). No one deserves to be mistreated online.

- **Lean on friends:** Friends are your lifelines. Share your experiences with them. They can provide emotional support and maybe even help you come up with strategies to deal with the bully (Patchin, 2017). I'm so glad I could be there for Amelia through this tough time. You're not alone, and your friends have your back.

- **Document everything:** If you ever need to take legal action or involve authorities, having a record of the bullying can be crucial. Save screenshots, messages, or any other evidence that might help if things escalate (Patchin, 2017).

- **Seek professional help:** If cyberbullying is causing severe emotional distress, consider talking to a counselor or therapist (Patchin, 2017). They are trained to help you deal with the emotional toll it can take.

Remember, you're stronger than you think. Cyberbullying is never okay, and you don't have to suffer in silence. Reach out to someone you trust, whether it's a friend, parent, or teacher, and let them know what you're going through. Together, we can stand up to cyberbullying and make the online world a safer and kinder place for everyone.

Digital Etiquette or Netiquette

Alright, let's start with the basics. Digital citizenship is like knowing the unwritten rules of the internet. It's all about being a responsible and respectful online citizen. Think of it as your superhero persona when you're online; you're out there to make the internet a better place.

Why Does Digital Citizenship Matter?

You might be wondering, *Why should I even care about all this digital citizenship stuff?* Well, here's the deal: the internet is like a huge playground, and we're all playing together. When we're good digital citizens, we make the playground awesome for everyone (*Digital Citizenship and Netiquette*, n.d.). But when we're not, things can get messy fast.

Respect and Netiquette – What's That?

Netiquette is just a fancy word for online etiquette. It's like having good manners for the internet. Imagine you're having a real-life conversation with someone. You wouldn't be rude, right? Well, the same goes for online chats, comments, and messages. Be kind and respectful, just like you'd want others to be with you (*Digital Citizenship and Netiquette*, n.d.). Here are some netiquette rules to live by:

- **Remember, there's a human on the other side:** Yep, even if you can't see them, there's a real person with feelings reading your messages.

- **Keep it real:** Be yourself online, just like you would offline. There's no need to pretend to be someone you're not.

- **Respect the vibe:** Different online places have different vibes. What's cool on TikTok might not be on a school forum. So, adjust your behavior to fit the vibe.

- **Don't be a Spammy McSpammer:** Avoid posting a zillion messages in a row or sharing unrelated stuff everywhere. It's annoying!

- **No drama, llama:** Don't start or feed online drama. It just creates negativity.

Your Digital Footprint – What's That About?

Your digital footprint is like your online legacy. It's all the stuff you do on the internet – the websites you visit, the things you post, and more. It's like leaving footprints in the sand; they don't just disappear (*Digital Citizenship and Netiquette*, n.d.). Colleges and future employers might check it out, so keep it clean and positive and remember these rules:

- **Think before you post:** Once it's out there, it's out there forever. Would you want your future college or boss to see it?

- **Privacy matters:** Don't share personal info like your address, phone number, or school. Keep it on the down-low.

- **Be a good friend:** Respect your friends' privacy, and don't share their secrets or embarrassing pics without their permission.

Copyright – What's Yours, What's Theirs?

Copyright is all about who owns what online. When you create something, like a cool artwork or a hilarious meme, it's yours, and you get to say how it's used. But you've got to respect others' work, too. Here's the scoop:

- **Say no to plagiarism:** Copying someone else's work and pretending it's yours is a big no-no. Always give credit where credit's due.

- **Understand fair use:** You can use someone else's stuff for educational or creative purposes, but don't go crazy with it.

- **No illegal downloads:** It might be tempting to grab that song or movie for free, but it's against the law. Support artists and creators by paying for their work.

Safety First – Guarding Against Hackers

Staying safe online is a top priority. Hackers and cyberattacks are real, and they can cause major trouble. Protect yourself with these tips:

- **Rock solid passwords:** Use strong passwords that are hard to guess. Mix it up with letters, numbers, and symbols. And don't share your passwords – ever!

- **Keep your guard up:** Be cautious about clicking on sketchy links or downloading shady files. If it looks fishy, it probably is.

- **Update and patch:** Keep your devices and software up to date. Updates often include security fixes.

- **Two-factor authentication (2FA):** Enable 2FA whenever possible. It adds an extra layer of protection to your accounts.

Brand Yourself – Your Personal Brand Online

Your online presence is like your personal brand. It's how people see you on the internet, and it can affect your future, especially when colleges and employers check you out. Tips for building a positive personal brand:

- **Stay true to you:** Be authentic and let your real personality shine through online.

- **Highlight your passions:** Share your interests and achievements. Let your passions be your superpower!

- **Show respect:** Be respectful and open-minded when interacting with others online. We're all unique, and that's a beautiful thing (*Digital Citizenship and Netiquette*, n.d.).

Taking Action – You Can Make a Difference!

The best part of being a digital citizen is that you can make a real difference. Here's how:

- **Stand up for others:** If you see someone being cyberbullied or treated unfairly online, be their hero. Speak up and report it.

- **Educate your pals:** Share what you've learned about digital citizenship with your friends. The more people who know, the better the internet becomes.

- **Be a role model:** Show others how to be awesome digital citizens by practicing what you preach.

Remember, being a digital citizen is not just about knowing the rules; it's about being kind, respectful, and responsible online (*Digital Citizenship and Netiquette*, n.d.). So, let's go out there and make the internet a place where everyone can thrive, learn, and have fun. We've got the power to keep it cool!

By the end of the week, Amelia's bullies were long gone, and life returned to normal.

Activity: Are You a Netiquette Pro?

Objective: To assess your own netiquette skills and identify areas for improvement in online communication.

Read each scenario below and imagine yourself in these situations. Assess how you would respond based on your understanding of netiquette. Rate your response on a scale of 1 to 5, with 1 being "Needs Improvement" and 5 being "Excellent." If you need help with giving yourself a rating, then suggest reaching out to an adult for help.

Scenarios:

1. You see a social media post that you strongly disagree with. How would you express your opinion in a respectful way?

2. You receive a text message from a friend with offensive language. What would you do?

3. You're in a group chat, and someone keeps sending unrelated memes. How do you handle this situation?

4. You want to share a funny video in a discussion forum. What

precautions would you take to ensure it's appropriate?

    5. You're joining an online gaming session with strangers. How would you introduce yourself and communicate with others?

Self-reflection: Take a moment to reflect on your ratings and responses. Identify areas where you feel confident in your netiquette skills (rated 4-5) and areas where you might need improvement (rated 1-3).

Goal setting: Set one specific goal for improving your netiquette skills. *For example, "I will think twice before posting a comment when I disagree with someone online."*

Action plan: Write down one action you can take immediately to work on your chosen goal. *For example, "I will pause and reread my comment before posting it."*

Wrap-up: Congratulations! You've assessed your netiquette skills and set a goal for improvement. Remember to practice good netiquette in your online interactions to create a positive digital environment. By completing this self-assessment, you'll gain insights into your netiquette strengths and areas that need attention. Setting goals and taking action will help you become a more respectful and responsible online communicator.

Chapter 3

Building a Positive Body Image in the Digital Age

Throughout history, the teenage years have been the most difficult when it comes to creating a positive body image. I know that grown-ups say that we always act like we are the first teens to ever go through teenage life even though it is something that every adult today had to go through in their time. But seriously! I don't think there has ever been a crazier era in the history of teenhood to rival this one. What am I talking about? The impact of this Digital Age and how to build a positive body image in spite of it.

Social Media and Self-Image

Seriously, it feels like Insta and Snapchat have more control over how we see ourselves than our own mirrors. But don't sweat it; i've got some insights to share (Solstice East, 2019).

So, here's the deal: social media can mess with our heads, especially us teen girls. It's not just about the mirror or our health anymore; it's about the social expectations that mess with our confidence and intuition. And guess what? Those Instagram influencers we follow sometimes have more say in how we should look and what we should do with our bodies than our own BFFs. Crazy, right?

Research even backs it up – spending too much time on social media can mess with our body image and lead to issues like disordered eating. Believe it or not, 88% of us compare ourselves to those perfect media images, and half of us feel negatively affected by it. Yikes!

But fear not, my friends; there are ways to tackle this. First things first, it's time to understand where all this low self-esteem comes from. Sure, we use social media to connect with pals and create our online personas, but it can also make us super conscious about how we look. Those comments about our appearance can sting, and suddenly, we're all about eating healthier – to the extreme, sometimes.

Now, studies say that girls who post tons of photos online and use filters to portray perfection often feel worse about their looks and develop serious food concerns. But the real deal here is that our self-esteem isn't just about our appearance. It's about feeling proud of our achievements and having awesome friendships, too.

So, what can we do to boost our body image and self-esteem? Well, for starters, let's remember that it's all about our mindset and how we see ourselves. No one's got a "perfect" body, and self-worth is about more than just looks. It's about rocking our individuality and being proud of who we are.

Next up, follow some body-positive accounts on social media. These peeps are all about self-love, trusting our bodies, and breaking free from those unrealistic beauty standards. Trust me, they're a breath of fresh air in a world filled with filters and photoshopped pics.

Now, let's chat about eating. Instead of obsessing over what we eat, let's focus on a healthy relationship with food. And hey, parents, it's time to set a good example by eating intuitively and not making negative comments about our bodies or what we munch on.

And you know what's cool? Enjoyable physical activities that make us feel awesome. It's not about hitting the gym to lose weight; it's about finding activities that bring joy. Think hiking, yoga, swimming, or self-defense – they're all about rediscovering the fun in movement.

Oh, and here's a pro tip: spending more time outdoors can keep us away from endless scrolling on social media. Win-win!

So, my fellow teens, let's remember – social media might have its grip on us, but we can take control of how we see ourselves. Self-worth isn't found in a filter; it's found in embracing our unique selves and being proud of it. Keep being awesome!

Overcoming Image Issues Created by Social Media

We all want to look our best, but social media can make us feel like we're falling short (Lai, 2022). It's not just about the influencers, though. There's this whole world of dieting and what the so-called "perfect body" should be. And let me tell you, it's everywhere. From the guilt-free recipes to the New Year's resolutions about losing weight, it feels like we're constantly bombarded with these messages.

But it's not just social media's fault. Diet culture has spread into every corner of our lives. It's this idea that being skinny equals being healthy and attractive. And it's so not true. Eating disorders are a real problem, and they affect people of all genders and identities.

Now, lawmakers are starting to take notice of these dangers. They're realizing that social media platforms need to step up and protect their users. They've even created fake accounts to see just how prevalent pro-eating disorder content is. It's like a wake-up call for all of us.

Pro-eating disorder communities have been around for ages, but they've found new life on social media. Despite all the rules and restrictions, these communities still thrive. People are finding ways to get around the algorithms and hashtags, making it harder for platforms to control.

But here's the good news: We can do something about it. Social media companies need to step up and take responsibility. They can't just rely on algorithms to filter out harmful content. We need more control over what we see on our feeds. Give us the power to mute certain keywords or even whole categories of content.

And hey, let's not forget about education. We can't just rely on social media platforms to fix everything. We need to promote body positivity in schools, in the media, and everywhere else. We need to spread the message that all bodies are good and worthy of love.

So, while social media might be part of the problem, it can also be part of the solution. It's time for us to take control of our feeds, our minds, and our lives. Let's create a world where we can all feel confident and happy, no matter what we look like.

Great Tips on Navigating the Social Media Maze

Navigating the social media maze can sometimes feel like wandering through a confusing labyrinth. But hey, we've got some tips to help us sidestep the eating disorder trap and come out stronger on the other side.

- **Know the signs:** First things first, educate yourself about the signs of eating disorders. Look out for sudden weight changes, skipping meals, or an unhealthy obsession with food and weight. If you notice any of these signs in yourself or a friend, don't hesitate to speak up. Awareness is the first step toward change!

- **Confidence:** Don't be afraid to open up and have a conversation about eating disorders with your friends or family. They're there to support you, and trust me, they've got your back. Sometimes, sharing your feelings can make all the difference.

- **Seek help:** If you suspect that you or someone you know might be dealing with an eating disorder, it's essential to reach out to a trusted adult. They can connect you with the right support and resources to get back on track.

- **Love yourself:** It's easy to get caught up in the comparison game on social media. But remember, you are unique, and that's what makes you beautiful. Embrace your individuality and always keep in mind that you're amazing just the way you are. No fancy filters required!

- **Stay balanced:** Forget about crash diets and extreme workouts. Instead, focus on maintaining a balanced and healthy lifestyle. Food should be enjoyed, not feared. Your body deserves nourishment and care.

- **Positive vibes:** Pay attention to your self-talk. Replace those negative thoughts with positive affirmations. Remind yourself that you're a rockstar and you've got what it takes to conquer anything life throws your way.

- **Support squad:** Surround yourself with friends who uplift and empower you. These are the people who'll be there to cheer you on through thick and thin. Your support squad is your secret weapon!

- **Chill out:** Stress can sometimes mess with our eating habits. So, find healthy ways to manage stress, whether it's through yoga, mindfulness meditation, or simply chatting with a friend. Let's kick stress to the curb together!

- **Stay informed:** Knowledge is power. Take the time to learn more about eating disorders and how to prevent them. The more you know, the better equipped you'll be to protect yourself and your friends.

- **Be patient:** Remember that recovery takes time, and it's entirely okay to have setbacks along the way. Celebrate every small victory, no matter how tiny it may seem. Progress is progress, and you're moving in the right direction.

Always keep in mind that you're not alone in this journey. We're all in it together, and together, we can stay healthy, happy, and confidently ourselves. You've got this, and you are beautiful just the way you are. Keep shining, you amazing rockstar!

Realizing the Power of Self-Acceptance

Reflecting on acceptance, especially during our rollercoaster teen years, is crucial. We all grapple with self-doubt and the hunger to belong and be acknowledged. It's like an invisible thread connecting us, tugging us toward recognition.

Being a teen is a wild ride. We're exploring our identity, craving independence, and sometimes pushing away from our folks while secretly needing their approval. It's a total paradox. I get it. But here's the kicker—research says our mental well-being hinges on how we see our parents accepting us (Lai, 2022). That's some serious parent power right there.

Feeling like you fit in and belong is gold for us teens. Sometimes, acceptance, even from sketchy peeps, feels like a lifeline to that sense of belonging. Walking away from iffy situations isn't always a breeze, even if they're not healthy.

The Body Image Struggle

It all boils down to body image – how we see ourselves versus society's standards. A negative body image can lead to unhealthy stuff like disordered eating.

Research says spending too much time on social media, especially on looks-related stuff, messes with our body image (Heger, 2022). We set unrealistic standards based on what we see, and when we can't meet 'em, it's like a punch to the gut.

Here's the kicker: constant comparisons. We see these "ideal" bodies and feel bummed when we don't match up. It's like we're stuck in an endless loop, thinking we're not good enough.

Photo Editing Pitfall

Editing pics should help, right? Wrong! It can make things worse. Most photos we see are edited to perfection. Filters and Photoshop create a fantasy world, making us think that's the norm.

Editing our own pics can be harsh. It magnifies our flaws, making us feel like everything needs fixing. But here's the twist – posting edited pics doesn't mess with us the same way. It might even boost our self-esteem a bit.

Choosing Who to Follow

Then there are "fitspo" and "thinspo" – accounts pushing us to be fit and thin. They make us feel like we're slacking. And it's not just a girl thing; guys feel the pressure, too, aiming for that ripped look.

But hold up, there's a silver lining. Social media ain't all bad. Some accounts scream body positivity. And guess what? They can boost our self-esteem. It's like a breath of fresh air, reminding us it's cool to be ourselves.

"Instagram versus reality" is a cool trend too. It shows that online images are often way different from real life. Seeing both sides reminds us nobody's perfect, and that's okay.

Revamping Beauty Standards

Listen, we're bombarded by society's body standards every day. Magazines, blogs, and TV tell us how we should look, eat, and feel. It's like swimming in a sea of crazy expectations.

But here's the deal: we don't have to let those messages define us. We can rebel and challenge toxic norms and own our self-worth. Here are five ways to stick it to society's body standards (Clegg, 2017):

- **Go on a media detox:** Ditch media that pushes body size, diets, and weight obsession. Is cold turkey too tough? Start small, drop one platform, or try a week detox. You'll feel liberated.

- **Dive into positivity:** Swap toxic sources for body-positive content. Books, blogs, movies, and docs celebrate all shapes and sizes. Focus on uplifting messages – what we focus on becomes our reality.

- **Rock affirmations:** Daily, find five things you're thankful for about yourself or your body. Quality beats quantity. Write 'em or meditate on 'em – affirmations reshape your self-image.

- **Try ACT (Acceptance and Commitment Therapy):** Accept that society shoved harmful thoughts into your noggin. Instead of fighting, acknowledge them as old news. Commit to kinder, true thoughts. Self-compassion and transformation, here we come!

- **Embrace nonjudgment:** In the world or watching TV, see beauty in all, no matter their size. If judgment creeps up, kick it—it's society's brainwashing. This practice lets you take back your view of beauty.

We can't flip society's script overnight, but we can start a self-revolution. We wake up daily to a world saying we're not enough, but we have the power to change that. We can live true to ourselves and see our worth through our own hearts.

Reclaiming your body image is a huge step to owning your true worth and kicking society's crazy standards to the curb. It's a rebellion worth starting today.

Media Literacy

Our school brought in a media whiz to drop knowledge on media literacy. She dished on how it, along with these mad skills, can help us rock a positive body image. Here's the juicy stuff she shared:

Understanding Media Literacy

First off, what's media literacy? It's not just knowing your way around tech; it's about being a boss at questioning the media stuff we consume (Rodgers, 2020). Think of it as giving the side-eye to what you see, hear, and read in media. 'Cause, spoiler alert: they're often cooked up by peeps with their own agendas.

Mad Media Skills

Here are some wicked media skills that are super handy:

- **Visual X-ray:** Media smarts taught me to see past the surface. We're talking about dissecting images to spot Photoshop, filters, and other image wizardry. It turns out those "perfect" bodies are often digital magic tricks.

- **Ad breakdown:** Media skills got me to break down ads by asking what they're selling and why. I learned to spot sneaky tricks like emotional hooks, celeb endorsements, and testimonials. Turns out, they're selling stuff by making us feel lacking.

- **Stereotype sleuth:** I also got good at spotting biases and stereo-types. It helped me see when media pushes harmful gender stereotypes or dreamy body ideals. That's when I decided to reject those toxic messages and demand more realness.

- **Truth detective:** Media literacy taught me to sniff out the real from the fake. When hunting for beauty and body info, I learned to tell the good sources from the sneaky ones.

- **Reality vs. fantasy:** One of my fave skills is comparing media to real life. Doing that, I realized the beauty standards in media don't match up with real peeps. That's when I started celebrating everyday beauty.

- **Content creator mode:** Media skills encouraged me to be a creator, not just a consumer. It's like peeking behind the curtain of media creation. This made me choosier about what I put out there, spreading positive body vibes online.

Finding Role Models

Media literacy also got me into finding and cheering on role models who rep body positivity. I dug up influencers, actors, and athletes who use their platform to spread self-love. Keeping these champs in my corner has been a game-changer.

Leveling Up Critical Thinking

Media literacy ain't just about body image; it's also about leveling up critical thinking. By questioning what I see and hear, I'm pretty much armor-plated against negative messages. I can spot when media's pushing unrealistic beauty, and I'm like, "Nah, not buying it."

Creating a Supportive Crew

Media literacy ain't a solo gig; it needs to be in schools and homes. Parents, teachers, and mentors can get the ball rolling by chatting about body image and media. These talks are safe spaces for us to vent and share.

My media literacy journey and these skills taught me this: positive body vibes aren't about fitting molds. It's all about rocking our unique beauty and knowing we're more than just looks. These skills let me flip the script on harmful messages, embrace diversity, and stand tall against media's pressure.

As a teen, I'm convinced that strong, updated media literacy and these survival skills are the secret sauce to owning a positive body image. Armed with media-slaying abilities and surrounded by body-positive role models, we can break free from society's unrealistic beauty norms and truly love ourselves.

Let's Get Media Savvy

Here's a short checklist on how to assess whether a media platform promotes positive body image and self-esteem:

- **Representation**: Does the platform showcase a diverse range of body types, ethnicities, and abilities? Are people with realistic appearances and imperfections featured?

- **Content themes**: Does the content emphasize the value of inner qualities, talents, and character over physical appearance? Is the content focused on promoting self-acceptance, self-love, and positive self-esteem?

- **Advertising and marketing:** Do advertisements avoid promoting unrealistic beauty standards and excessive photo editing? Are ads and sponsored content aligned with positive body image messages?

- **Engagement and interaction:** Does the platform encourage constructive and supportive discussions rather than body shaming or negativity? Are users empowered to report or block harmful content or users?

- **Inclusivity:** Is the platform inclusive of individuals from different backgrounds, genders, and identities? Does it actively combat discrimination and hate speech?

- **Content moderation:** Does the platform have clear content guidelines and policies against body shaming, bullying, and harmful behavior? Is there a transparent process for reporting and addressing such issues?

- **Educational resources:** Does the platform provide educational materials or resources on body image, self-esteem, and mental health? Are there experts or professionals who contribute to discussions on these topics?

- **User feedback and reviews:** Are there positive testimonials or reviews from users who have found the platform supportive of their self-esteem and body image? Are there any patterns of negative feedback or criticism regarding these issues?

- **Privacy and security:** Does the platform prioritize user privacy and data protection to reduce the risk of cyberbullying or body image-related harassment?

- **Transparency:** Is the platform transparent about its stance on promoting positive body image and self-esteem? Does it openly address any controversies or concerns related to these topics?

By assessing a media platform using this checklist, we can make informed decisions about whether the platform aligns with our values and supports a healthy self-image and self-esteem.

Activity: Daily Affirmations

Choose and repeat the following affirmations daily or whenever you need a boost of self-confidence. These affirmations are specifically tailored for you to help improve your acceptance of your body and physical appearance. Consistent practice can help shift your mindset toward greater self-acceptance and appreciation.

- "I love and accept my body just as it is right now."

- "My worth is not determined by my appearance; I am valuable just as I am."

- "I choose to focus on the things I love about myself, inside and out."

- "I am unique and beautiful in my own way."

- "My body is strong and capable, and I am grateful for all that it does for me."

- "I release the need for comparison and embrace my individuality."

- "I am more than my physical appearance; I am a kind, intelligent, and compassionate person."

- "I nourish my body with love and care, providing it with the care it deserves."

- "I celebrate my flaws as part of what makes me beautifully imperfect."

- "I am confident and comfortable in my own skin."

- "I am deserving of self-love and self-acceptance."

- "I choose to see beauty in diversity, including within myself."

Chapter 4

MAPPING YOUR PATH TO SUCCESS

"When I was fifteen, I had my whole life planned out. I knew exactly what I wanted to do, and I went out there and did it!" says Dad, puffing up like he's the hero of his own story as he messes up my hair like I'm his long-lost son.

Ugh! I can't stand these father-daughter heart-to-hearts!

But deep down, I know Dad's got a point. Supposedly, I should have my act together by now, but honestly, I don't. It won't be long before I'm drowning in college applications and life-altering decisions about my future career. It's stressing me out big time.

This chat with Dad made me realize I needed to get my act together and talk to some people who actually know what they're talking about – definitely not my Dad!

So, I set up a meeting with our school's guidance counselor, Ms. Bennet. She turned out to be awesome and helped me figure out my path to self-discovery.

I love how Ms. Bennet cuts through all the psych talk and gets real about what actually works. She said that the secret to finding the right career is to walk a fine line between what I love doing and what I am great at – sometimes they are not the same thing. She advised me to work on identifying my passions and interests.

Most importantly, Ms. Bennet emphasized that this journey should be an ongoing conversation. We should talk about my experiences, my excitement, and my reflections. It's through these discussions that my passion can grow and evolve.

So, there you have it – what I learned from my heart-to-heart with Ms. Bennet. It's time to set sail on the sea of possibilities, guided by my newfound passion. Who knows where this journey will lead me, but one thing's for sure: it's going to be an epic adventure!

Career Options Quest

Imagine the career world as a massive galaxy, and you're the daring astronaut ready to explore (Indeed Editorial Team, n.d.). Here are some tips:

- **Know thyself:** Start by figuring yourself out. What gets your heart racing? What do you rock at? What's your treasure map? Write it down.

- **Go big:** Don't limit yourself! Check out all kinds of careers, from artsy stuff to science to starting your own gig.

- **Research galore:** Dive deep into your dream careers. What skills and knowledge do they demand? Think about getting a degree, some training, or cool certifications.

- **Goal setting:** Time to create your roadmap! Set goals for your studies and career path. Plot your course through this cosmic journey.

- **Study success:** Your spaceship to success is through academic excellence! Here's how to unlock your full academic potential (Indeed Editorial Team, n.d.):

    ○ **Pick your path:** Choose the educational journey that matches your career dreams, whether it's a degree, apprenticeship, or vocational training.

    ○ **Stay on target:** It's a long haul, but stay focused. Attend classes, study hard, and don't hesitate to ask for help.

    ○ **Love Learning:** Don't just cram for tests; embrace the joy of learning. Curiosity is your bestie on this voyage.

- **Extracurricular adventures:** Explore activities, clubs, or internships related to your field. These add some oomph to your knowledge.

- **Exploring personal interests, passions, and hobbies:** It is said that if you do what you love for a living, you will never work a day in your life. When exploring what you are good at, try pursuing your interests, passions, and hobbies to unlock your unique gifts and talents.

There you go – your guide to navigating the galaxy of career choices. Buckle up; it's going to be an out-of-this-world journey!

Your Toolbox of Skills

In addition to exploring your passions and interests, it would also help your career prospects to develop your leadership, time management, and communications skills and brush up on your public speaking.

Leadership Skills

Have you ever wondered what it takes to become an inspiring leader? Well, look no further because we've got the inside scoop on the essential skills that can transform any teen into a motivational leader (*6 Secrets to*

Becoming an Inspiring Teen Leader!, 2023)!

1. **Stand up for your values:** Inspiring leaders are like superheroes when it comes to doing what's right. They have strong values, like honesty and kindness, and they back up those values with action. Imagine being the first to stand up for a friend who's getting teased about their appearance – that's the spirit! So, take a moment to reflect on your own values and ensure that your actions align with them. If you ever need guidance, don't hesitate to have a chat with a trusted adult.

2. **Respect and fairness rule:** Awesome leaders are humble and exceptional listeners. They respect everyone's viewpoint and ensure that everyone's voice is heard. They embrace diversity and challenge stereotypes because they believe every individual has something valuable to offer. Empathy, or the ability to understand how others feel, is their secret weapon.

3. **Lend a helping hand:** True leaders make their mark by helping others. It can be as straightforward as reading to a younger child or lending a hand to a classmate struggling in a subject where you excel. You can also join a club or volunteer at a shelter. Making a difference feels fantastic!

4. **Be a role model:** Leaders lead by example. They set goals, make wise choices, and stay committed to their dreams. They don't let peer pressure sway them, and they learn from their mistakes. You can do this, too! Establish your own goals, have faith in yourself, and rise above any drama that comes your way.

5. **Encourage others:** Leaders guide others toward success. They inquire about people's aspirations, assist in crafting plans, and connect them with mentors or valuable resources. Start by actively listening to your friends and classmates, and encourage them to contemplate their goals. Let them know you have faith in their abilities!

6. **Learn from the best:** Inspiring leaders draw inspiration from others and seek mentorship and support. Who inspires you? Maybe it's a teacher, a coach, or a trustworthy adult. Don't hesitate to reach out to them for guidance and support to supercharge

your leadership skills.

There you have it, future leaders! These six tips are your secret recipe for becoming an inspiring teen leader. Share these insights with your friends, and watch your leadership squad grow!

Time Management Skills

It might sound boring, but trust me, it's the secret sauce that can turn your high expectations into reality. Let's face it, at the start of each semester, we're full of ambition and dreams of acing our studies. But without a solid plan, those dreams can fizzle out like a deflated balloon. Time flies, and if you're not careful, the end of the semester will sneak up on you, leaving you feeling unprepared and overwhelmed.

In all of my research, I discovered a simple yet powerful time management strategy to help us stay on track and excel in our studies (sbrands, 2021):

Step 1. Prepare a term calendar: At the beginning of each term, before the academic storm hits, create a term calendar. This calendar should cover the entire term and include (*Using Effective Time Management to Improve Your Studying*, 2019):

- Assignment due dates

- Test dates

- All school activities

- Extracurricular commitments

The big-picture view of your term sets the stage for successful time management.

Step 2. Prepare a weekly schedule: Your weekly schedule is your compass for each week of the term. Every Sunday, sit down and plan your week. Here are some of the things to include:

- List your classes for each day.

- Refer to your term calendar and add items due or happening during the week.

- Review your previous week's notes and schedule to see if anything carries over.

- Include extracurricular activities from your term calendar.

- Note down when you'll tackle assignments, study sessions, or group projects.

Step 3. Prepare a daily schedule: Now, let's break it down even further. Each evening, create a daily schedule for the following school day. As you complete tasks, mark them off. Here's the daily drill:

- Transfer tasks from your weekly schedule to your daily one.

- Note any unfinished tasks from the previous day.

- Check for any new school activities in your daily plan.

- Add any other commitments from your weekly schedule.

Managing your time is more than just having calendars and schedules. It's about making the most of every minute. Here are some additional time management tips (sbrands, 2021):

- **Prioritize:** Start with the toughest or most important task first. Tackling the big challenges while you're fresh and focused makes the rest of your studies feel like a breeze.

- **Find your space:** Don't waste time looking for a study spot. Find a dedicated, distraction-free space where you can concentrate.

- **Create study blocks:** Break your study time into blocks of around 40 to 50 minutes. Take short breaks in between to recharge.

- **Schedule wisely:** Put schoolwork first. Schedule other activities for after your studies to avoid last-minute stress.

- **Use resources:** Don't be afraid to seek help from friends, tutors, study groups, or the Internet when tackling complex subjects.

- **Stay healthy:** Exercise, eat well, and get enough sleep. A healthy body and mind boost your efficiency.

- **Stay flexible:** Unexpected obstacles happen. Be flexible, but always get back on track.

Time management might seem like a chore, but it's your golden ticket to success. With a well-organized plan, you can make the most of your time and achieve your academic goals. Remember, the clock is always ticking, so let's make every second count.

Communication Skills

Communication skills might not sound like the most thrilling thing to master, but trust me, it's a superpower you'll need in high school, college, and beyond. So, here are cool tips to level up your communication game (Crevin, 2020)!

- **Be a listening pro:** Ever heard the saying, "Listen more, talk less?" Well, it's gold! When someone's talking, give them your full attention. Ask questions if you're unsure, and don't multitask – no texting while chatting!

- **Know your audience:** Imagine you're chatting with your BFF versus texting your teacher. Big difference, right? Tailor your language and tone to match who you're talking to. No "LOLs" in professional emails, okay?

- **Master body language:** Did you know your body talks too? When chatting in person or on video, keep those arms uncrossed and maintain eye contact. On video calls, look into the camera, not at yourself on the screen.

- **Proofread like a pro:** Before you hit send, double-check your messages. Spellcheck can be sneaky. Make sure your words say what you intend. And always read the whole message before replying.

- **Take notes, seriously:** Just like in class, take notes during conversations. It helps you remember stuff and shows you're organized. Plus, sending a follow-up email is a pro move.

- **Make the call:** Sometimes, it's better to pick up the phone, especially if you've got loads to say. It allows for a more natural conversation.

- **Think, then speak:** Before you blurt out your thoughts, take a moment. Think about what you want to say and how to say it respectfully. You'll sound mature and thoughtful.

- **Smile and stay positive:** Believe it or not, even on the phone, your attitude shines through. Smile and be positive – it makes people respond in a friendly way.

So, there you have it, communication champs! These tips may not turn you into a superhero overnight, but they'll definitely help you rock those conversations, whether you're chatting with friends or future bosses. Keep smiling and keep communicating!

Overcoming Your Fear of Public Speaking

We've all heard it before – the fear of public speaking is pretty darn common. In fact, surveys say that around 72–75% of people get the jitters when it comes to speaking in public. But hey, no worries because we're here to spill the beans on how to become a confident speaker using what we like to call the three magical Ps: Purpose, Preparation, and Practice (Souers, 2022).

First things first, why bother overcoming the fear of public speaking? Well, for starters, it can unlock doors to academic and professional success. Think about it: you'll likely have to give presentations in school (hello, oral reports) and maybe even take a college public speaking class. Plus, being a confident speaker is like a superpower for leadership, and who doesn't want that on their resume?

- **Purpose – Find your why:** Let's start with the first "P" – Purpose. Imagine you're in a video game, and you've got a mission. Having a purpose makes everything more exciting, right? It's the same with public speaking. It's way more motivating when you're talking about something you care about and have a purpose for sharing.

- **Preparation – You can't skip this step:** Now, for the big one – Preparation. This is where the fear-busting magic happens. Think of it like preparing for a big quest in a role-playing game. You've got to plan your journey. Start with research, create outlines, and draft your speech or presentation. Knowing exactly what you want to say and how to say it is key. Also, consider visual aids and props if they fit your presentation. They're like power-ups in your speech! They can help you remember what to say without needing a script.

- **Practice makes (almost) perfect:** Lastly, let's talk about the third "P" – Practice. Practice doesn't mean you have to memorize everything word-for-word. It's about rehearsing your speech until it flows naturally and you've got the intro, main points, and conclusion down pat. Try practicing in front of a mirror, recording yourself, or even presenting to friends and family. The more you practice, the more confident you'll become.

4-H: Your Public Speaking Playground

If you're up for a challenge, consider joining 4-H contests like Public Speaking and Demonstrations/Illustrated Talks. These events are like leveling up your public speaking skills. You'll have a chance to show off your newfound confidence and maybe even win some cool prizes!

So, with Purpose, Preparation, and Practice, you'll be well on your way to conquering your fear of public speaking and rocking those presentations. Remember, it's not about being perfect; it's about being yourself and sharing your awesome ideas with the world. Game on, fearless speakers!

How to Land Your First Job

Check out these awesome tips to help you rock that job hunt and land your first real job (Hackett, 2023):

1. **Create your first resume:** Yep, we know you might think a resume is for fancy grown-ups, but hear us out – it can make you stand out! Even if you don't have job experience, showcase your educational achievements and community involvement. Think of it as your "I'm awesome" document.

2. **Gather your docs:** Now, you'll need some official stuff. Get your social security number sorted, and if you don't have a driver's license, grab a passport or photo ID. Depending on your state's

rules, you might need your parent or guardian to sign off on your job quest.

3. **Dress to impress:** First impressions count! Dress up when you're applying for jobs. Show those employers that you mean business. A professional look says, "I'm ready to work hard."

4. **Nail the interview:** Practice makes perfect! Prep your answers to common interview questions. Use examples from school or extracurricular activities to show off your skills. Remember, confidence is your secret weapon.

5. **Apply Everywhere:** Don't put all your eggs in one basket. Apply online and in person. Walking into a place to apply can make a big impression. But don't ignore those online job listings – they're a goldmine!

6. **Embrace rejections:** Bummer alert: Rejection happens. But don't let it get you down. Keep your chin up, and don't take it personally. Each rejection brings you closer to your dream job.

7. **Network, girl!:** You might not have a bunch of connections yet, but don't be shy. Ask friends and family about job openings. You never know who might know someone hiring. Networking is a game-changer!

8. **Send a thank you note:** A little politeness goes a long way. After an interview, send a thank-you note or email. It shows you're respectful and thoughtful. You're not just a great worker; you're a great person.

9. **Time management is key:** Balancing work and school is a juggling act. Keep the lines of communication open with your employer about your school commitments. Your education should always come first.

10. **Stay positive and keep going:** Job hunting can be tough, but stay positive. It's a learning experience, and you might make a few mistakes. Remember, the right job is out there, and patience will lead you to it.

Now, get out there and conquer the job hunt, future superstar! Your first job is just around the corner. Here are a few online sites you can try (Hearn, 2022):

- **Snag:** Formerly known as Snagajob, Snag is a fantastic tool for teen job seekers. While anyone can use it, Snag has a dedicated section designed for teenagers. It allows you to search for jobs by zip code and categorizes them as full-time, part-time, or teen-specific, making it easy to find the right job at a glance.

- **Hire Teen:** Hire Teen is tailored to teenage workers and offers jobs in various categories. Teens can search by keyword, city, state, and age or specifically look for jobs in their age range. It includes positions like food service, camp counselors, dishwashers, and even modeling jobs for teens. These entry-level jobs can be valuable for building experience that will benefit them in the future.

- **Teens4Hire:** Teens4Hire is a site designed to help those aged 14 to 19 find seasonal, volunteer, or part-time jobs. High schoolers need to register for an account, while employers also register to list jobs online. Teens4Hire also provides information and tools for interview preparation and office etiquette. Recruiters can use the site to find prospective employees, and it's run by an organization dedicated to helping teens.

- **Survey Junkie:** For those who prefer something other than traditional employment, Survey Junkie offers an interesting solution. Teens can sign up, create a profile, and get matched with surveys that fit their profiles. Completing surveys earns them points, which can be redeemed for PayPal or gift cards. This platform also offers information on monetizing social media accounts and seeking self-employment.

- **Summer Jobs:** As the name suggests, Summer Jobs connects people with seasonal work opportunities. It's perfect for teens who might not qualify for jobs in other fields, and it's an easy way to find jobs as a lifeguard, summer camp counselor, babysitter, or lawn mower for local businesses.

- **Nextdoor:** Nextdoor is a social media platform that's divided by neighborhoods and zip codes. To utilize it, you need to prove you live in a specific area. If extracurricular activities or other responsibilities interfere with a traditional job search, Nextdoor can help you find odd jobs within your community to earn some extra cash.

- **Fiverr**: Fiverr is an online freelance platform where individuals can offer various services, from drawing and animation to programming and writing. It's a great option for teens since the minimum age requirement is only 13, unlike other freelance platforms like Upwork. Freelance work can help build a strong portfolio, which can be beneficial when applying for more traditional job positions in the future. In a world where traditional job openings might not always align with the specific jobs teens are looking for, freelance options provide flexibility. Moreover, they allow teens to develop a portfolio that can be a valuable asset in their future job searches.

So, there you have it – a list of websites to help you kickstart your careers, gain valuable experience, and earn some money along the way. With these options, there are no more excuses for not finding the perfect job to match your interests and goals. Happy job hunting!

College Application Tips

So, you might be about to dive into the wild world of college applications, and let's face it, it can be as nerve-wracking as trying to untangle earphones that have been sitting in your pocket for a week. But fear not because we've got some tips that will help you conquer this epic quest (Mom, 2023)!

- **The early bird gets the worm:** Starting early is like discovering the cheat codes to the college application game. It gives you time to research colleges and mark those all-important deadlines. Plus, you won't end up sweating over essays at the last minute like you do with math homework.

- **Be the organization wizard:** Imagine your college application as a treasure hunt. You'll need a map (your plan), a backpack (your materials), and a sense of direction (staying organized). Create a system to keep track of everything. It's like creating your own magical spell for success.

- **Truth Is your best friend:** When filling out those applications, honesty is your superpower. No need to inflate your achievements like a superhero's ego. Just be yourself, and colleges will appreciate your authenticity.

- **Customize, customize, customize:** Think of each application as a personalized potion for each school. Show how your interests and goals match each college's vibe. It's like trying to impress a different character in a video game by offering them the right gear.

- **Rec letter magic:** Time to call in the cavalry! Ask your favorite teachers or mentors for recommendation letters early. Be sure to give them enough time to whip up those magical words.

- **Spell check is your sidekick:** Your application is like a superhero's cape; it has to be flawless. So, proofread it like your life depends on it. No typos allowed!

- **Submit before the deadline monster attacks:** Missing deadlines is like facing the final boss in a video game without the right gear. Make sure to submit your applications on time to avoid any game-over moments.

- **Keep your eyes on the prize:** After you've submitted your applications, don't just sit back like a sleepy cat. Follow up with the colleges to make sure they've received everything they need. It's like checking your pizza delivery status to make sure it's on its way!

- **Interview showdown:** Some schools love interviews. Prepare by researching the school and practicing answers to common questions. Think of it as leveling up your communication skills!

- **Be the explorer:** Lastly, remember, it's not just about one college. Keep an open mind and explore different options. Think of it as trying out different video games; you might discover a hidden gem!

With these tips, you'll be well on your way to conquering the college application adventure with style, humor, and a smile. Remember, this is your chance to shine and show colleges why you're the hero they've been waiting for. Game on!

I can't say that I'm a model student, and the road to academic excellence is paved with long hours and intense discipline. Keeping our eyes on the prize can be challenging at our impressionable age. But that is just one of the reasons why it is crucial to surround yourself with a strong support system of friends, family, mentors, and role models. Finding your tribe is more important than just hanging out with the right crowd or not succumbing to peer pressure (not to be taken lightly); it could actually impact your long-term plans in more significant ways than you may think.

Activity: Dream Job Collage

Creating a career vision board can be an exciting and motivating way to set and achieve those goals. It's a visual representation of where you want to be professionally and can help you stay focused on your aspirations.

What is a Career Vision Board?

A career vision board is like a creative collage that helps you set intentions and stay focused on your dream career. It's a powerful tool that combines images, words, and representations to remind you of your professional goals and inspire you to take action (Hebert, n.d.).

What Should a Career Vision Board Include?

Your career vision board should be a reflection of your career goals and aspirations. Here are some key elements to consider including (Hebert, n.d.):

- **Career goals:** Clearly define your career goals on your vision board. Whether you aspire to become a doctor, an artist, a programmer, or anything else, include images or words that represent those goals.

- **Inspirational images:** Add images that inspire and motivate you. These can be photos of successful people in your field, your dream workplace, or any visual that represents your ideal job. These images should make you feel excited and determined.

- **Affirmations:** Incorporate positive affirmations that resonate with your goals. Affirmations are powerful statements that reinforce your belief in yourself and your abilities. For instance, use phrases like, "I am capable of achieving my dream career" or, "I am on the path to success."

- **Skills and qualifications:** Include elements representing the skills and qualifications you want to acquire or already possess. If you're aiming to improve your coding skills, for instance, add coding-related images or the word "coding" to your board.

How to Create a Career Vision Board

Now, let's walk through the steps to create your career vision board:

1. **Decide on the format:** You can choose between a physical or digital career vision board. A physical board involves cutting out images and words and pasting them onto a board or canvas. A digital board is created using online tools like Canva, Pinterest, Google Slides, or PowerPoint. The choice depends on your preferences and resources.

2. **Find images and words:** Gather images and words from magazines, books, and online platforms, or create your own. Make sure they align with your career goals and resonate with your aspirations.

3. **Arrange images and words:** Start arranging the elements on your vision board, being intentional about their placement. Experiment with different layouts until you're satisfied with the overall look and feel.

4. **Personalize your vision board:** Add personal touches to make your vision board unique. Include images or words that have special meaning to you or represent your unique journey. This personalization adds a personal touch to your board.

What is Your Career Vision? Examples and Ideas

Your dream career is all about your personal goals, interests, and aspirations. So, let's talk about how to create a career vision that's perfect for teen girls like you. Here are some ideas and examples to get you started:

- **Pursuing your passion:** Is there something you absolutely love doing? Your career vision can be all about turning your passion into a job. If you're into art, for example, your vision board might be filled with pictures of artists, their work, and the colors and designs that inspire you.

- **Exploring new horizons:** Maybe you're curious about different fields or industries. Your vision board can help you explore your interests. If you're considering a career change, gather images and words that represent those new possibilities.

- **Achieving milestones:** Think about specific achievements you want in your career. It could be winning a scholarship, getting a summer internship, or even starting your own business. Your vision board can be a collection of images and quotes that push you to reach those goals.

Creating a career vision board is a creative and exciting way to set and chase your career goals. It's like having your dreams right in front of you, reminding you to stay motivated and focused. Your vision board is your personal map to success, showing you the way to your dream career.

Remember, it's your career journey, and your vision board is your unique guide. So, let your creativity flow, and start building your career vision board today! Your dream career is out there, waiting for someone as amazing as you to chase it.

Chapter 5

SELF-ESTEEM SUPERCHARGE AND MASTERING BOUNDARIES

Cross-legged at Aunt Moira's, the tea's aroma wafting, I sought guidance for my heartache.

"Emily," Aunt Moira began gently, "relationships are puzzles, pieces needing a fit. Amelia and Grace are crucial parts of your puzzle, but they're clashing."

My two besties, caught in a war between popular cliques, wanted me to pick sides – what a mess!

"I don't want to choose, Aunt Moira. It feels like a betrayal."

Aunt Moira comforted me. "Building self-esteem is key, Em. Know yourself and your values, and build self-confidence."

"So, find my true self?" I asked.

Aunt Moira nodded. "Explore passions, set goals, and embrace boundaries."

"How do I set boundaries without being rude?" I questioned.

"We'll work on that. Assertive communication is vital," Aunt Moira said.

"What about toxic relationships?" I asked.

"Watch for red flags and seek support when needed," Aunt Moira advised.

"Family dynamics can be tricky," I said.

Aunt Moira chuckled. "Effective communication and managing conflicts are key."

Taking a sip of tea, I felt empowered. "I want strong family bonds."

Aunt Moira patted my knee. "With the right tools, you'll create beautiful connections."

Aunt Moira's wisdom guided me, and I even found some tips to share. You can thank me later!

Building Self-Esteem for Epic Relationships

Have you ever noticed how folks clash sometimes? It's like accidentally poking a beehive when you didn't even know it was there. Well, a lot of times, it's because of this thing called self-esteem, the secret sauce of relationships. Yup, that's right, this ain't just grown-up talk – it's your day-to-day mojo!

So, what's the deal with self-esteem, you ask? Well, it's basically how you feel about yourself. Think of it as your personal confidence-o-meter. It can be sky-high one day and basement-level the next (Prinsloo, 2022). And guess what? That's perfectly normal! Self-esteem's like your mood – it can swing like Tarzan.

Healthy self-esteem is like loving your pet, even when they turn your kicks into chew toys (Prinsloo, 2022). It's all about embracing yourself, warts and all. Imagine being your own BFF – pretty rad, huh?

Leveling Up Your Mental Game

Boosting self-esteem isn't just about feeling good; it's like an XP boost for your mental health. If you're tackling stuff like anxiety or feeling blue, working on your self-esteem's a game-changer (Prinsloo, 2022). It amps up your sense of worth and helps you steer the stormy seas of emotions.

One sweet perk? High self-esteem makes you treat yourself like royalty. Picture showing yourself kindness, like you would to your pals. When you're your own cheerleader, good vibes ripple out to everyone else.

But beware of negative self-talk – it's like self-esteem's kryptonite (Prinsloo, 2022). It zaps your mood and makes you feel like a sidekick. Yeah, life throws curveballs, but during those funky times, remember to be your own MVP.

Lonely, Misunderstood, and Introverted

I totally get what it's like to be an introverted and sometimes lonely teen. It can feel overwhelming at times, but trust me, you're not alone in feeling this way.

First of all, it's essential to remember that being introverted is not a flaw; it's just a part of who you are. Embrace it! Finding your people might take time, but it's worth the effort. Start by joining clubs or groups that align with your interests. It's easier to connect with people who share your passions. Online communities can be fantastic, too.

Don't be afraid to initiate conversations; sometimes, all it takes is a simple "hello." And remember, quality over quantity when it comes to friends. It's perfectly fine to have just a few close buddies. Lastly, don't hesitate to reach out to a trusted adult or a counselor if loneliness becomes overwhelming.

You're stronger than you think, and there's a world of possibilities waiting for you out there. Keep your head up!

Self-Esteem: Your Relationship Wingman

Self-esteem's not just a solo act; it's like the star player in life's playbook, influencing everything. Seriously, it's your squad's captain, your emotional guru, and your hype-up artist all in one (Cherry, 2021).

Four Mighty Powers of Solid Self-Esteem

- **Skills and swagger:** Healthy self-esteem's like knowing your superpowers and flexing them with confidence. It's like having a secret stash of swagger.

- **Rock-solid bonds:** If you vibe with yourself, you'll vibe with others. Healthy self-esteem's your VIP pass to epic connections.

- **No capes needed:** You don't gotta be a superhero 24/7. Real self-esteem's all about setting achievable goals – no costume changes required.

- **Speak your truth:** Imagine letting your needs fly without a care. That's the gift of strong self-esteem – you're a ninja communicator, and your voice counts. You practice mindfulness and gratitude as part of your existentialist truth.

Balancing Act of Self-Esteem

Now, here's the scoop: Low self-esteem might make you doubt yourself, pull iffy moves, and feel unlovable. Not the vibes we're chasing, right? It can even wreck relationships and drag you into a pit of negativity (Cherry, 2021).

On the flip side, mega-high self-esteem might make you think you're untouchable, like a superhero with no chinks in the armor. But, let's face it, nobody's flawless. Sky-high self-esteem can mess with growth 'cause you're all about staying perfect (Cherry, 2021).

The Expert Take

Psychologists like Abraham Maslow, the guy who made that famous hierarchy of needs pyramid, say self-esteem is a big deal. It's like needing both outside appreciation and inner self-respect to reach your full potential. You know, like a combo move in a video game (Cherry, 2021).

But hold up, self-esteem isn't the same as self-efficacy, which is all about how you think you'll handle future stuff. Self-esteem is like your overall self-worth, while self-efficacy is about your confidence in specific tasks (Cherry, 2021).

What Shapes Your Self-Esteem

Lots of things can influence your self-esteem. We're talking about your age, genetics, physical abilities, and even the way you think about things. Life experiences play a massive role too. So, if you've had a lot of negative vibes from friends or family, that can affect your self-esteem (Cherry, 2021).

Oh, and let's not forget about the big bad bullies – racism and discrimination can also mess with your self-esteem (Cherry, 2021). But hey, don't forget, you have the power to shape your self-esteem too.

Healthy Versus Low Versus Excessive Self-Esteem

Healthy self-esteem: You're not stuck in the past, you believe you're equal to everyone else, you express your needs, you're confident, you're a glass-half-full kind of person, and you know your strengths and weaknesses (Cherry, 2021).

Low self-esteem: You think others are better than you, you struggle to express your needs, you focus on your weaknesses, you battle self-doubt, you see the world through gray-tinted glasses, and you're scared of failure.

Excessive self-esteem: You might be a perfectionist, you always want to be right, you feel entitled to success, you believe you're the best at everything, and you're kinda full of yourself.

How to Give Your Self-Esteem a Boost

Okay, so you might be wondering, *How do I level up my self-esteem game?* Here are some quick tips (Cherry, 2021):

- **Spot negative thoughts:** Recognize those sneaky negative thoughts that creep in and try to bring you down.

- **Challenge negativity:** When you catch those thoughts, challenge them with more realistic and positive ones. It's like being your own cheerleader!

- **Positive self-talk:** Practice saying positive things to yourself. You've got this!

- **Be compassionate:** Forgive yourself for past mistakes and accept all parts of yourself. Nobody's perfect, and that's what makes us awesome.

Remember, having healthy self-esteem isn't just about feeling good; it's the key to reaching your goals, setting boundaries in relationships, and staying grounded in who you are. So, go out there, rock that self-esteem, and build some amazing relationships – starting with the most important one: your relationship with yourself.

Emily's Top Self-Esteem Tips

I'm sharing some awesome tips to help you boost your self-esteem and confidence. We all want to feel great about ourselves, right? So, whether you're a teen like me or someone else, these tips are for you (biglifejournal.com, 2022). Let's dive in!

- **Love yourself unconditionally:** Guys, it's crucial to know that your worth doesn't depend on your grades, looks, or anything else. You're amazing just as you are. Even when things go south, or you make mistakes, remember that you're still worthy of love.

- **Embrace a growth mindset:** Sometimes, we might think we can't change or grow. But guess what? Our brains are incredible, and we can totally improve. So, let's chat about the growth mindset. It's all about seeing potential and learning from everything we do.

- **Don't fear failure:** Mistakes happen, and they're actually pretty cool because they teach us stuff. So, if you mess up, don't stress. Talk it out with friends or family, and ask yourself, "What can I learn from this? How can I do better next time?"

- **Celebrate the process, not just the outcome:** When you achieve something, it's not just about the result; it's about the hard work, effort, and determination you put in. So, pat yourself on the back for the journey, not just the destination.

- **Learn new skills:** If you're struggling with something new, that's totally fine. We're all growing, and it's okay to face challenges. Look for opportunities to practice and get better at what you're passionate about.

- **Be persistent:** Sometimes, you might not feel super confident about trying new things, but that's alright. Keep going, and you'll gain confidence along the way. Remember, it's okay to take on new challenges even if you're not 100% sure about them.

- **Reassure yourself:** Life can be a rollercoaster, and it's okay to make choices that are right for you, even if they're tough. Remind yourself that growing up and changing is normal. You're not a bad person for outgrowing certain things or people.

- **Nail assertive communication:** Being a clear and confident communicator is a superpower. Learn how to express yourself without being passive or aggressive. Practice in front of a mirror, work on your body language, and speak with confidence.

- **Practice at home:** Home is the perfect place to practice your communication and social skills. Role-play different scenarios with friends or family to prepare for real-life situations.

- **Show self-compassion:** Don't be too hard on yourself. Growing up can be tough, but it's all part of the journey. Try mindfulness or positive affirmations to boost your self-esteem. Treat yourself with the same kindness you'd show a close friend.

- **Explore different interests:** Get involved in various activities and hobbies. It helps boost your self-esteem because you'll find value in different areas of your life. Plus, it's fun to discover new passions.

- **Share advice sparingly:** While it's tempting to give advice, sometimes it's better to let your friends figure things out themselves. Encourage them to think through challenges and find their own solutions. It helps them become more confident in handling problems.

- **Ask for advice:** Don't be afraid to open up to friends about your own challenges. It shows that you're human and that you're learning and growing, too. Sometimes, your friends might have great insights to share.

- **Be a good listener:** Sometimes, your friends just need someone to listen, not to preach or lecture. Try to understand their point of view, and don't rush to judge. Sometimes, empathy is more important than offering solutions.

- **Believe in yourself:** You're watching, and you're learning from your experiences and the people around you. So, remember to handle challenges with confidence and practice self-love. It's all about growth and improvement.

Building self-esteem and confidence takes time, but with these tips, we can all become stronger and more self-assured individuals. We've got this!

With all this focus on your own self-development and journey, I expect that there will be much less time to get into trouble over what other teens in your circle are doing. And if you find that someone is taking an unhealthy interest in your life, perhaps it is time to discuss the importance of setting boundaries (I am still learning to do this, too).

All About Boundaries

Understanding boundaries is super important, not just for avoiding bad relationships but also for taking care of your mental and emotional well-being (*Being Assertive and Setting Boundaries*, 2020). It's a two-way street, though – respecting others' boundaries is just as crucial. Boundaries aren't walls; they're like bridges connecting us with respect, self-worth, and realness. Strong women set various types of boundaries, from personal to emotional, and they know their worth.

To get others to respect your boundaries, you've got to communicate assertively. Find a win-win solution, use assertive communication, and know your boundaries well. When someone crosses your boundaries, calmly but firmly express your feelings, specify the behavior, state your boundary, and suggest how they can respect it. It's important to remember that "no" is a valid answer in healthy relationships, and respecting others' "no" is essential too.

When dealing with tricky conversations or peer pressure, stay polite but firm, express doubt if needed, and offer alternatives. Handling feedback gracefully is also essential for personal growth. If someone violates your boundaries, stay calm, acknowledge their feelings, express care, restate your boundaries, find common ground, state consequences if necessary, and take a break if things get heated. Your safety and well-being come first, always, and it's perfectly okay to stand up for yourself and maintain your boundaries. You've got this!

Setting Personal Boundaries Helps Relationships Thrive

The only hobby some folks in my friend circle seem to be interested in these days is the ongoing tiff between my besties. As you already know, I'm smack dab in the middle of a showdown between my two BFFs, Grace and Amelia. Drama alert! So, what did I do? I went on a little research spree about setting personal boundaries. And guess what? It turned out to be a total game-changer, not just for me but for sorting out the whole Grace vs. Amelia mess (Gordon, n.d.).

Feelin' my feels: First off, I found out that recognizing my own feelings is a big deal. Like, seriously, who knew emotions could be so tricky to pin down? But here's the deal: Knowing what's going on inside is key to knowing when and where to draw those boundary lines.

Trust your gut, girl!: Oh, and trust your gut, peeps! Sometimes, things feel off even when you can't put your finger on it. It's like your inner compass knows what's up, even when your brain is like, "Huh?" So, yeah, trust your instincts, even if others are all like, "Nah, that's not right."

Spotting the no-nos: I did some digging on spotting those no-no behaviors in other peeps. You know, what's cool and what's not in relationships. Turns out tolerating unhealthy stuff isn't the way to go. No one's got time for that, right?

Screens and schemes: In today's tech world, digital boundaries are where it's at. I got the lowdown on digital etiquette, the whole sexting deal, and how to deal with digital drama. Keeping it real online is a must!

Phrases to drop: And here's the juice: having some epic phrases in your toolkit can be a lifesaver. Try out stuff like, "Let me think about that and get back to you," or "I'm not vibing with that." Trust me, these come in clutch when dealing with tricky situations or peer pressure.

Practice makes perfect: Turns out practice is key! I realized that working on my boundary-setting skills in a chill family setting is a smart move. Saying "no" when you need space or can't handle more stuff? Totally legit.

Friendship vibes: Also, I learned that not every friend needs to be your everything. Friends are like a mixed bag of Skittles – different flavors, ya know? It's cool to have different opinions and beliefs; that's what makes things interesting.

Lead by example: Oh, and if you want others to respect your boundaries, you gotta show 'em how it's done. I started setting boundaries in my own life, cutting ties with anyone who didn't treat me right, and just putting self-respect first.

Pressure Cooker Situations

Sometimes, it feels like everyone's pushing you to do something you're not cool with. Peer pressure is real, and it can mess with your head. But remember, it's okay to say "no."

Handling Pressure on the Spot

Quick tips when you're feeling pressured (*Being Assertive and Setting Boundaries*, 2020):

- Be polite but firm.

- Express doubt politely.

- Buy some time.

- Offer an alternative.

- Put the ball in their court.

- Distract with humor.

- Reassert your boundary.

Receiving Feedback

Feedback can be tough, but it's a chance to grow. Take your time to process it. Don't take it personally; it's about your actions, not you as a person. Be grateful for it, and if you need to, apologize and show growth (*Being Assertive and Setting Boundaries*, 2020).

Remember, you're not alone in this. Reach out to friends, family, or professionals if you need help along the way. You've got a whole bright, beautiful future ahead of you, and toxic relationships are so last season!

As for my BFFs, like a storm in a teacup, time – not to mention the stressful mid-term tests – got everyone back to normal a few days later!

Activity: Peer Pressure Decision Tree

Use this decision tree when you face peer pressure to help you think through your choices, potential consequences, and alternatives.

1. **Peer pressure situation:** Describe a situation or decision where you feel peer pressure. *For example, you and your friends are at a party, and some of them suggest trying alcohol, even though you're underage.*

2. **My initial reaction:** Write down your initial thoughts or feelings about the situation. *For example, you feel a mix of excitement and anxiety. You want to fit in, but you're aware it's against the law.*

3. **Options:** List the possible choices you have in this situation. *For example, join your friends and have a drink, politely decline and explain your reasons, or suggest doing something else fun at the party.*

4. **Consequences:** Consider the potential consequences of each option. *For example, getting caught by parents or authorities, deciding not to drink but your friends might be disappointed, or doing the alternative option which your friends find fun and strengthens your friendship.*

5. **Values and priorities:** Reflect on your personal values and priorities. Which option aligns best with what matters most to you?

For example, your values might include honesty, integrity, and following the rules. Your priority might be staying out of trouble and maintaining your reputation.

6. **Alternative solutions:** Are there alternative choices that neither succumb to peer pressure nor go against your values? *For example, suggest playing a fun party game or dancing or offer to be the designated driver.*

7. **My Decision:** Choose the option that you believe is the best for you in this situation.

8. **Reflection:** After making your decision, reflect on how it felt, what you learned, and whether it aligned with your values.

Remember, it's okay to seek guidance from a trusted adult or friend when dealing with peer pressure. Your choices should ultimately reflect your own values and well-being.

Chapter 6

THE PUBERTY ADVENTURE AND TAKING CARE OF YOURSELF

Picture this: I'm in my room, jamming to music, doing my teen thing, when my little sis, Hannah, barges in with the big questions. She's all curious about puberty, and honestly, I'm not sure how to explain it without making it sound like a science lecture.

Hannah's firing off questions like it's a rapid-fire quiz. "Why do period cramps hurt so much?" "Why am I suddenly hosting a pimple party on my face?" And I'm there, headphones off, feeling like I'm trying to explain quantum physics to a goldfish. It's a tough one.

So, I decided it was time to figure out how to have these talks with Hannah in a way that's not boring or embarrassing. We're diving deep into the world of those changes that turn you from a kid into a full-blown teenager. Get ready for this rollercoaster!

Why Puberty?

Puberty is like the transformation from a caterpillar to a butterfly but with way more drama. It happens anywhere from age 8 to 14, but there's no set schedule for it. Your brain sends bossy texts (hormones) to different body parts, telling them to gear up for the puberty show.

For guys, it means testosterone, sperm, hair down there, surprise erections, and even the occasional "wet dream." Plus, say hi to voice cracks and voice dropping and, yes, even some breast growth (the weirdest superpower ever, right?). Don't worry; the chest thing usually sorts itself out.

Ladies, your journey starts with "buds" under your nipples, which will grow into breasts. You'll also get your ticket to the pubic hair party and some extra curves as your hips widen. Aunt Flo makes an appearance about 2 years after those buds arrive. And don't forget the emotional rollercoaster – thanks, hormones!

Emotions and Puberty

So, about those hormones – they're not just messing with your outsides; they're having a wild dance party on the inside, too. You might feel like your emotions are on a rollercoaster ride. Anxious, angry, confused – you name it, puberty's got it.

It's okay if this all sounds a bit weird. The important thing is to know that it's normal. If you can't chat with your folks or me about it, there are other people you can turn to, like doctors, school nurses, teachers, or counselors. They've heard it all before, trust me.

Oh, and here's a secret: Everyone goes through puberty at their own speed. So, if your BFF seems like a supermodel while you're still feeling like a kid, no worries. You're unique and fabulous, just as you are, inside and out.

So, there you have it, the thrilling, sometimes wacky world of puberty.

Buckle up, 'cause this ride's just getting started!

Physical Changes During Puberty

Emily: Hey, look, Hannah, I get it. You're on the puberty curiosity train. Well, buckle up because I'm your guide to this wild rollercoaster called adolescence! Puberty might sound like a sci-fi movie, but guess what? It's happening to us right now. So, get ready for some fun facts and a whole lot of awkwardness (Raising Children Network, 2017)!

Hannah: Oh, I'm ready, Em! But, like, what even is puberty?

Emily: Puberty, my dear Watson, is the magical time when our bodies decide it's time to grow up. It's like our bodies throwing a massive party, and everyone's invited! Inside and out, everything's changing, and it's totally natural. So, no worries!

Hannah: Okay, so when does this epic journey start?

Emily: Ah, the million-dollar question! Puberty usually kicks in when we're around 10-11 years old for girls and 11-12 years old for boys. But brace yourself, it can start anywhere between 8 and 13 years for girls and 9 and 14 years for boys. Basically, our bodies are like, "Time to level up!"

Hannah: Wow, that's a wide range! What are the cool changes happening, Em?

Emily: Well, darling, let's talk about the ladies first. Picture this: You wake up one day, and boom, your breasts have decided to make an appearance! Around 10-11 years, breast development is like the opening act of puberty. It's normal for them to grow at different speeds, and hey, they might even be a bit tender. And guess what? If you want a bra, go for it! Comfort is key.

Hannah: So, you're saying my problem is normal?

Emily: (Nodding) Yep, totally!

Hannah: Yay! Okay, what else?

Emily: Oh, hold on, there's more! Get ready for a growth spurt! Some parts of our bodies, like our heads, faces, and hands, might grow faster than others, making us look a bit wonky for a while. But don't worry; we usually stop growing at around 16-17 years old.

Hannah: What about the guys?

Emily: Boys get their turn, too! Around 11-12 years old, their genitals start growing – yes, that includes the penis, testes, and scrotum. And oh, pubic hair decides to join the party, too, getting darker and thicker over time. Fun, right?

Hannah: Totally! But what's with the awkwardness and clumsiness?

Emily: Ah, the clumsy phase! As our bodies grow, our balance takes a hit. It's like suddenly having longer limbs but not knowing what to do with them. So, expect a bit of extra stumbling and bumbling for a while. We're basically puppies learning to talk!

Hannah: Haha, got it! Anything else?

Emily: Oh, absolutely! Get ready for the surprise guest appearances: acne and body odor! Thanks to active skin glands, our faces might break out a bit. And you know that funky smell? Yep, that's body odor, courtesy of our new sweat glands. But hey, a little deodorant goes a long way!

Hannah: Puberty sounds both crazy and fascinating!

Emily: You bet it is! Puberty is like our bodies' way of saying, "Hey, time to grow up and embrace the awesome changes!" So, don't worry, sis. We're all in this together, and it's going to be one heck of a ride!

That Time of the Month – Menstruation

A few days after our cute heart-to-heart discussion, Hannah crawled into my bed one afternoon. Her period pain was pretty bad, and she needed some TLC. "Why do we have to go through all this pain and bleeding in the first place, Sis?" moaned Hannah, scrunching into the fetal position.

I thought the best way to distract Hannah from her pain would be to give her a little biology talk mixed with some big-sisterly advice on hygiene and self-care – suddenly, the sense of responsibility I felt for my little sister seemed pretty heavy. If I didn't teach her how to handle herself, who would? Mom and Dad are so wrapped up with climbing the corporate ladder that they're never around for the important stuff.

I got a heating pad for Hannah and then settled into our little chat (Health-wise Staff, 2022).

"Alright, imagine your body has this cool baby-making superpower, and it's always preparing for the possibility of creating a tiny human. Now, I'm not saying it's time to give up your V-card, Hannah. No way! I'm talking about biology here, nothing else."

"As if, Em. Boys, ew!" responded Hannah with a groan.

"Once a month, your uterus decides to spruce up its walls, just in case a fertilized egg decides to move in. Think of it like redecorating your room but on a whole different level!

But, if Mrs. Egg doesn't meet Mr. Sperm, or if they meet but don't hit it off, your uterus is like, 'Well, time to hit the reset button!' That's when the lining it built up gets a one-way ticket out and then hello, period!"

"Why do I have to put up with this every month?" wailed Hannah. I dipped into my secret stash of goodies and pulled out her favorite candy bar. She looked like she could do with a good dose of chocolate.

"Now, don't freak out if yours isn't like clockwork. Periods are kinda like the weather; they can be a bit unpredictable. On average, it lasts about 3 to 5 days, but remember, everyone's body is different, so don't stress if yours doesn't match the textbook.

Oh, and speaking of stress, it can make your periods a tad worse. So, try to relax, maybe binge-watch your favorite TV show, or eat some chocolate – it's like medicine for the soul, trust me!"

"Mmm! Thanks for sharing from your secret stash, Em. It's so good!" mumbled Hannah, her mouth filled with chocolate.

"No problem. I know the pain all too well – it can be a real party pooper, right? And how about those mood swings? You can try a warm water bottle on your belly (it's like giving your uterus a cozy hug) or lie down with a pillow under your knees. Exercise is another trick – it gets your blood pumping and can help with the pain. And if things get really intense, you can ask the doc about some over-the-counter pain meds."

"Now, let's talk about what to wear during this whole extravaganza. We've got options! Tampons, pads, and even menstrual cups – it's like a fashion show for your lady parts. Tampons are like those sleek sports cars, pads are your trusty minivan, and menstrual cups are like eco-friendly, reusable magic cups. You can even go swimming with tampons or menstrual cups, which is pretty rad!

Just remember, change them regularly, or you might end up with an unexpected show. And we definitely don't want that!

So, there you have it, Hannah! The lowdown on Aunt Flo's visits and how to handle them like a champ. Don't let it get you down; it's just another chapter in the exciting adventure of growing up!"

I think that between the cozy heating pad, the chocs, and my great company, Hannah finally dozed off to sleep.

Personal Hygiene

For extra credit in sociology class, we had to create a vlog presentation about personal hygiene for teenagers. After doing a bit of research and loads of scripting and planning, this is the transcript of my presentation (Patwal, 2014):

Why Should Teens Be Hygienic?

Personal hygiene for teenagers is kind of like that secret ingredient in a recipe. You might not think much of it, but it can make or break the dish. Trust me; I've had my fair share of "cooking" up personal hygiene habits over the years, and it's been quite the journey.

So, why should we teens care about personal hygiene? Well, here's the scoop. Think of it as our magical shield against the forces of ickiness. I mean, no one wants to be buddies with germs, right? And let's be honest, being known as the "Stinky Steve" or "Funky Fiona" in school is not the reputation we're going for.

Hair Care

Teenagers are like tornadoes of activities, which means our hair can become a dirt magnet. Plus, thanks to those lovely hormones, it can get all oily and smelly. So, regular hair washes with a mild shampoo and a sprinkle of hair magic, and I'm good to go.

Nail Care

Sure, long, fancy nails are cool, but they're like germ hotspots! They can host a germ party and invite them into your mouth, nose, and eyes. Yikes! A nail brush is my hero, and I trim them weekly to avoid ingrown nails.

Oral Care

Bad breath and tooth decay? No, thank you! Flossing once a day and flashing my pearly whites with fluoride toothpaste twice a day keeps my smile in check.

Handwashing

Now, onto handwashing. My hands are like tiny explorers, touching everything. So, I make it a game – washing my hands before and after meals, after playing with pets, and especially after using the bathroom. Trust me; germs are the ultimate hide-and-seek champs.

Bathing

Bathing is a lifesaver, especially when you're dealing with those lovely puberty sweat glands. They create a perfect recipe for body odor! So, showers are my go-to after any physical activity. Antiperspirant or deodorant, anyone?

Toilet Hygiene

Toilet hygiene is an oldie but a goodie. Wiping the right way and keeping it clean is crucial. No one wants a germ party down there!

Menstrual Hygiene

Now, for my fellow teenage girls, menstrual hygiene is a must-know. Tracking periods, using the right products, and disposing of them safely are all part of the game.

Shaving

Shaving is another fun chapter. Boys and girls, be careful and use the right tools! And remember, no sharing!

Clothes and Shoes

Clean clothes and shoes are the cherry on top. Changing clothes daily, especially undergarments and socks, keeps the germs at bay. Plus, it's like a mini makeover every day.

In a nutshell, personal hygiene is like our suit of armor against germs and the awkwardness that puberty brings. So, fellow teens, let's embrace it, stay fresh, and keep our hygiene game strong! Your future self and friends will thank you.

Those Pesky Pimples

For her vlog, Grace was assigned the topic of acne. Since I helped her put the presentation together, I get to share it with you, with her permission. This is what Grace had to say about acne – its causes, management, and treatment (Cohen, 2021).

Greetings, I'm Grace, your friendly neighborhood skincare aficionado, and I'm here to unveil the ultimate anti-acne skincare regimen. Yes, I know the struggle – acne can be a real buzz-kill. But worry not because we've got the inside scoop on tackling those troublesome pimples.

First things first, acne doesn't play favorites – it's not just a teen issue. Adults can also find themselves in the acne club! Hormones, stress, and even some sneaky ingredients in your beauty products can all conspire against your skin. But fret not; we're armed with a well-structured plan.

Let's break it down step by step as if we're crafting the recipe for perfect skin. Think of me as your guide, and we've got some expert tips from the pros – top dermatologists who are essentially the chefs of skincare. They've concocted a recipe for clear skin that's so straightforward that even a skincare novice like me can follow it.

- **Step 1. Gentle face wash – morning freshness:** Picture your face as if it were a delicate silk blouse. You wouldn't go scrubbing it like you're cleaning muddy sneakers, right? That's the secret here. Start your day with a gentle foaming cleanser – it's like a refreshing wake-up call for your skin. If you've got a spot treatment or prescription acne medication, let them sit this one out for now.

- **Step 2. Application of acne treatment:** If you went for the mild cleanser in the morning, this is your time to shine! After your face is dry, apply over-the-counter acne medication to those pesky spots. Patience is your ally; it typically takes around six weeks to see results. If the pimple party is still going strong on your face after that, don't hesitate to consult a dermatologist for some extra firepower.

- **Step 3. Non-greasy moisturizing magic:** Moisturizer might seem like an unnecessary step when you're battling oil, but guess what? It helps regulate oil production and keeps your skin well-hydrated. Opt for oil-free, noncomedogenic moisturizers – they're like a refreshing gulp of water for your skin.

- **Step 4. Sunscreen – your skin's shield:** Sunscreen is non-negotiable, my friends! Choose one that won't clog your pores or aggravate breakouts. A reliable sunscreen is like a trusty umbrella, shielding your skin from UV damage and ensuring it stays healthy.

- **Step 5. Nighttime cleanse – bid adieu to the day's grime:** In the evening, it's time to gently bid farewell to all the make-up, oil, and grime that your face has collected during the day. A surfactant-free cleanser is your go-to here. If you're into toners, make sure they're oil-free. And why not treat yourself to a double cleanse with micellar water followed by your cleanser? It's like the cherry on top!

So, my fellow acne warriors, here's the deal: stay patient and committed to your skincare routine. Clearing and fading those blemishes takes time, much like mastering a new dance move. It won't happen overnight, but trust the process! However, if you feel the problem is severe, please consult your dermatologist for professional advice.

Now, let's flaunt our radiant, acne-free skin with confidence. Who's ready to rock it?

Exercise

As Amelia and I huddled around her laptop, we had a cunning plan. Our goal? To convince our parents to let us enroll in the new local health club that had just opened. With visions of us showing off our super-fit bodies and rubbing shoulders with the in-crowd, we embarked on our mission.

Emily: (With a mischievous grin) Amelia, we've got to make this convincing. Our parents need to see that exercise isn't just for sweaty gym rats; it's for cool teens like us!

Amelia: (Nodding enthusiastically) Totally, Em! Let's start by showing them how exercise can make us feel good. Like, it's the ultimate mood booster.

I quickly pulled up an article titled "Why Exercise Is Wise" in Spanish, and Amelia began translating it into English (Gavin, 2018).

Benefits of Exercise

Amelia: (Giggling) Oh, check this out! Exercise makes us feel good because it releases chemicals like endorphins that are like happiness grenades in our brains. Boom! Goodbye, grumpy teenage mood swings!

Emily: (Laughing) Exactly, Amelia! And it helps us sleep better. You know how we're always complaining about staying up late watching Netflix?

Amelia: (Rolling her eyes) Ugh, yes. Exercise can be our secret weapon against binge-watching. But what about this one? Exercise lowers the chance of depression and anxiety.

Emily: (Grinning) Oh, they'll love that! It means fewer dramatic teenage meltdowns. We'll be like zen masters.

Disease Prevention

Amelia continued translating, and we reached the part about preventing diseases.

Amelia: (Excitedly) Em, check this out. Exercise can help us keep a healthy weight and lower the risk of diseases like diabetes and heart problems.

Emily: (Pretending to be alarmed) Diabetes? Heart problems? We can't let that happen, Amelia! We need to stay fit and fabulous.

Aging

Amelia then moved on to the section about aging well.

Amelia: (With a dramatic gasp) Emily, we're not thinking about wrinkles and grey hair now, but exercise can help us age gracefully! It's like the fountain of youth.

Emily: (Feigning seriousness) Absolutely, Amelia. We'll be forever young, and our parents will be so proud.

Types of Exercise

With the benefits of exercise outlined, we moved on to the types of exercises we could do.

Amelia: (Raising her eyebrows) Em, we need to make them see that exercise isn't just about lifting weights. We can have so much fun with it!

Emily: (Nodding) Totally! We can do dance, swimming, and even hiking! Let's make them think we're going on exciting adventures every day.

Amelia finished translating the article and looked at me with determination.

Amelia: (Fist pumping) Alright, Em, we've got the facts. Now, let's add a little pizzazz and tell them it's like joining a secret teen club where we'll be the coolest members.

Emily: (Winking) Oh, they won't be able to resist! We'll tell them we need exercise buddies to keep us motivated, and we might even meet cute gym crushes!

As we finalized our plan, Amelia and I couldn't help but burst into laughter. We knew our parents would soon be convinced that enrolling us in the new local health club was the best idea ever.

Amelia: (Grinning) Em, we've got this! We're gonna be the fit and fabulous teens we were born to be!

Emily: (High-fiving Amelia) You bet, Amelia! Operation "Convince Our Parents to Let Us Join the Health Club" is a go!

Healthy Eating

Basically eating healthy fuels your body with the right stuff, helping you stay energetic, focused, and ready to take on the day. It's like your secret weapon for feeling great and doing your best in everything you tackle!

I guess we got so hyped up about our plan to join the gym that we didn't even think that our folks might turn us down. They basically laughed in our faces and were like, "You girls won't get fit with all the junk-food you eat!" Challenge accepted, right?

So, we did some intense research (read: Googled stuff) to come up with the ultimate healthy eating meal plan that'll make our parents eat their words. Here's what we found in our quest to get those #GymGoals:

According to the Eatwell Guide (2015), we're supposed to eat stuff from five main food groups. Yeah, yeah, sounds boring, but it's essential. These groups are like our food squad:

- **Fruit and vegetables:** Like, duh, salad is a thing.

- **Starchy foods:** Potatoes, bread, pasta, all that carby goodness.

- **Proteins:** Think fish, lean meat, eggs – the stuff that gives you muscles.

- **Dairy:** Milk, cheese, yogurt – basically, the cool kids of the food pyramid.

- **Healthy oils and spreads:** For some healthy fats. Avocado toast, anyone?

Key Nutrients

Now, they're talking about iron, vitamin C, calcium, and vitamin D, all the stuff we need to be actual superheroes:

- **Iron:** You get it from meat, fish, and, like, dark green veggies (who knew?). If you're a vegetarian, fortified cereals (but check the sugar content) and stuff can give you a hand.

- **Vitamin C:** You need some vitamin C buddies with your iron-rich veg, 'cause they help each other out. Aside from your citrus fruit, even cauliflower, broccoli, bell peppers, and tomatoes contain vitamin C too.

- **Calcium:** Milk, yogurt, and cheese – they're all in for strong bones. Also, don't forget about canned fish with bones (sounds kinda fishy, but it's true).

- **Vitamin D:** The sun is your bestie for this one, but if it's hiding, consider a supplement. Just remember to wear good sun protection when you're outside for longish periods.

What Foods to Avoid

The fun part (not). We've gotta try say no-no to:

- **Fatty, sugary, salty stuff:** Small amounts, guys, don't go overboard.

- **Fast food:** It's like, "See ya, burgers and fries!"

- **Energy drinks:** Not for us, peeps under 16. Too much caffeine can mess with our chill vibes.

- **Processed foods:** Try whole food options in place of overly processed foods (out of a package).

Meal Plan

Here is the healthy meal plan Amelia and I put together from all the research we had done.

Breakfast Options:

1. Scrambled eggs with spinach and whole-grain toast: 2 scrambled eggs, a handful of fresh spinach, 1-2 slices of whole-grain toast.

2. Greek yogurt with berries and a drizzle of honey: 1 cup of Greek yogurt, 1/2 cup of mixed berries, and a drizzle of honey.

3. Oatmeal topped with sliced bananas and a sprinkle of nuts: 1 cup of cooked oatmeal, 1/2 sliced banana, and a tablespoon of chopped nuts.

Morning Snack Options:

1. Sliced apple with peanut butter: 1 small apple with 2 tablespoons of peanut butter.

2. Carrot sticks with hummus: A handful of carrot sticks with 2-3 tablespoons of hummus.

3. Low-fat cheese with whole-grain crackers: 1-2 ounces of cheese with a serving of whole-grain crackers.

Lunch Options:

1. Grilled chicken or tofu salad with mixed greens and vinaigrette dressing: 3-4 ounces of chicken or tofu, a large salad with mixed greens, and 2 tablespoons of dressing.

2. Whole-grain wrap with turkey, avocado, and veggies: 1 whole-grain wrap with 3-4 ounces of turkey, sliced avocado, and various veggies.

3. Lentil soup with a side of whole-grain bread: 1 bowl of lentil soup with 1-2 slices of whole-grain bread.

Afternoon Snack Options:

- Sliced cucumbers with a yogurt-based dip: A cup of sliced cucumbers with 1/2 cup of yogurt-based dip.

- Trail mix with a combination of nuts, seeds, and dried fruits: A small handful (about 1/4 cup) of trail mix.

- A smoothie made with banana, spinach, Greek yogurt, and a touch of honey: 1 smoothie with a 6-ounce serving of Greek yogurt and a reasonable portion of the other ingredients.

Dinner Options:

1. Baked salmon with quinoa and steamed broccoli: A 3-4 ounce salmon fillet, 1/2 cup of cooked quinoa, and a side of steamed broccoli.

2. Stir-fried tofu with brown rice and mixed vegetables: 4-6 ounces of tofu, 1/2 to 1 cup of cooked brown rice, and a generous portion of mixed vegetables.

3. Grilled lean beef or a veggie burger with sweet potato fries: 3-4

ounces of lean beef or a veggie burger, a small serving of sweet potato fries.

Evening Snack (if needed):

1. A small bowl of mixed berries: 1/2 to 1 cup of mixed berries.

2. Cottage cheese with a drizzle of honey: 1/2 to 1 cup of cottage cheese with a drizzle of honey.

3. Air-popped popcorn with a sprinkle of nutritional yeast: A small bowl of air-popped popcorn with a light sprinkle of nutritional yeast.

These portion sizes are general guidelines, and individual needs may vary. It's best to listen to your body's hunger and fullness cues and adjust portion sizes as needed. If you have specific dietary requirements, consider consulting a registered dietitian for personalized guidance.

Getting Enough Zs

I totally get it – being a teenager can sometimes feel like a sleepless adventure, but let's talk about the importance of getting enough shut-eye and how we can catch those much-needed Zs (Canadian Paediatric Society, 2008).

Raise your hand if you've ever struggled to stay awake during a boring History class. Yep, been there! Or maybe you've had those dreaded Monday mornings when getting out of bed feels like an impossible mission. Oh, and let's not forget those afternoon nap attacks that hit us like a ton of bricks as soon as we walk through the door after school. If you nodded your head to any of these, you're not alone. Many of us teenagers feel like we're running on empty most of the time.

So, why are we always so darn tired? Well, part of it is because we're growing like weeds. Our bodies, minds, and emotions are going through some serious turbo-charged changes, which means we need more sleep than when we were kids and even more than we will when we become adults. Scientific research says we should be getting about 9 to 10 hours of sleep each night.

Now, you might be thinking, "What's the big deal about sleep?" Well, let me break it down. Lack of sleep can seriously mess with your game, affecting things like memory, concentration, and the big one – motivation. When you're tired, even getting out of bed can feel like climbing Mount Everest. Plus, it can lead to mood swings and even depression. I'm not kidding, folks; this is some serious stuff.

So, why is it so tough to get enough sleep? Well, some of it's in our control, and some of it isn't. Many schools start way too early (seriously, who decided 8 a.m. was a good idea?), and we've got homework, sports, chores, part-time jobs, and a ton of other stuff on our plates. Finding time to catch those Zs can be a challenge. We've got busy lives, and some of us might even be overscheduled – meaning we're running around like headless chickens, leaving no room for relaxation and sleep.

But fret not, my friends, I've got some tips that might help you get the rest you need:

- **Bedtime routine:** Set up a relaxing bedtime routine. Sleep in your bed, not in front of the TV. Make sure your room is cool, dark, and quiet.

- **Weekend wake-up:** Try to wake up within 2 to 4 hours of your usual wake time on weekends, even if you stayed up late the night before.

- **Hours in bed:** Aim for at least 8 hours in bed each night, but many of us need 9 to 10 hours to stay awake during the day.

- **Consistent schedule:** Go to bed at roughly the same time every night.

- **Morning light:** Let the sunshine in as soon as you get up in the morning.

- **Exercise:** Get some physical activity every day, but avoid intense workouts in the evening.

- **Check your schedule:** Are you overscheduled? Make sure you have time for fun and sleep. You don't want to be a zombie.

- **No caffeine afternoon:** Steer clear of caffeine after midafternoon, no matter how much you love your coffee or energy drinks.

- **Daytime naps:** Avoid napping during the day, but if you must, keep it short, less than 30 minutes, and don't nap after dinner.

- **Bed is for sleep:** Use your bed for sleeping only, not for homework, TV, or phone chats.

- **No sleep aids:** Avoid using any products to help you sleep, including alcohol, herbal stuff, or over-the-counter sleep aids.

Following these tips should help most of us teens get enough sleep to feel more alive during the day. But if you're still feeling tired all the time or experiencing other issues, it might be time to see a doctor.

So, if you've got unshakeable sadness, constant worries, trouble falling asleep, or if you wake up in the middle of the night and can't get back to dreamland, or if you feel like a lifeless zombie despite getting enough sleep, it's time to seek some professional help.

Remember, getting enough sleep is crucial for our well-being and success as teens. It's not just about feeling awake in class; it's about being our best selves, staying safe on the road, and keeping our mental health in check. So, let's make sleep a priority and conquer the world, one well-rested night at a time!

Bra-Fitting 101

Since it seemed like reaching our fitness goals was gonna take more than a minute, we decided to go the retail therapy route of self-care. So, me and my BFFs, Grace and Amelia, decided to go on a shopping spree to find the right dress style to match our body types. We also brought along my mini-me, Hannah, 'cause she's on a mission to conquer the world of bras for the very first time.

To us, this wasn't just any shopping trip; it was an adventure of epic proportions – a quest to find the perfect drip to show off our unique body shapes and help Hannah take her first steps into the world of big-girl undergarments.

Now, Hannah's still in that phase where she thinks unicorns are real and broccoli is evil, so this was gonna be quite the experience for her. And guess who got to be her trusty sidekick on this mission? That's right, yours truly, Emily, the bra-fitting expert (well, kinda).

So, before we strutted our stuff into that lingerie store, I had to prep Hannah on what to expect. Here's the lowdown, straight from my expert-ish perspective *(Kirsten, 2018)*:

- **It takes longer than you think:** Hannah, being her adorable self, thought this whole thing would be, like, five minutes tops. But, girl, it took way longer. We needed like 20-30 minutes. And we didn't even rush. Lesson learned. Never try to squeeze this in at the last minute!

- **You will have to take your top off:** I know, right? A bit of a shocker, but it's a necessity. The pros at the store need a clear shot to measure you properly. But don't fret; they have these fancy fitting rooms, and you're the only star of the show in there!

- **You may not be the size you expect:** So, Hannah was pretty confident about her size (like most of us), but turns out she was a little off. It happens to the best of us. Our bodies change, and so do our bra sizes. Don't sweat it, Hannah; it's all part of the process.

- **You will have to talk about your boobs:** Hannah blushed at this one, but honestly, it's no biggie. The fitter knows their stuff, and they need the deets to find the perfect fit. So, you chat about your girls for a bit, and boom, you're on your way to bra nirvana.

- **You will learn new things about bras:** This part was kinda cool. The fitter schooled us on all the bra facts we never knew. Seriously, there's more to bras than meets the eye. We even got a mini-lecture on bra styles. It was like Bra 101 in there!

There are various bra styles to cater to different body types and fashion preferences. There is the t-shirt bra, known for its seamless and versatile design; the cleavage-enhancing balconette for those who want to amp up their cleavage; the plunge bra, perfect for deep V-neck tops and dresses; the confidence-boosting push-up bra, ideal for those with smaller breasts; and the must-have sports bra for maximum support during high-impact activities.

Activity: Journaling Journey

Welcome to your Journaling Journey, a personal space where you can explore and express your thoughts and emotions during this exciting phase of adolescence. Follow these steps to make the most of your journaling experience:

Step 1. Choose a Journal:

- Find a journal that resonates with you. It could be colorful, plain, or have inspiring quotes.

- Make it your own – decorate the cover, add stickers, or personalize it in a way that feels uniquely you.

Step 2. Set the Scene:

- Create a comfortable and quiet space where you can journal without distractions.

- Play soft music, light a candle, or add any elements that help you relax and focus.

Step 3. Start with Reflection:

- Begin each journaling session with a moment of reflection. Take a few deep breaths to center yourself.

- Consider how you're feeling physically, emotionally, and mentally.

Step 4. Prompts for Exploration:

- Use prompts to guide your writing. Here are some ideas to get you started:

  - How did you feel today?

  - Are there any new experiences or challenges you faced?

  - What are you grateful for today?

     ○ Describe a moment that made you proud.

Step 5. Express Yourself:

- Don't worry about grammar or perfect sentences. Let your thoughts flow freely.

- Use drawings, doodles, or stickers to add a creative touch to your entries.

Step 6. Track Changes:

- Record physical changes you notice during puberty. This might include growth spurts, skin changes, or anything else on your journey.

- Note your evolving emotions and how you're learning to navigate them.

Step 7. Celebrate Achievements:

- Acknowledge and celebrate your achievements, no matter how small. It could be mastering a new skill, handling a challenging situation, or simply expressing yourself.

Step 8. Be Honest and Open:

- Your journal is a judgment-free zone. Be honest about your feelings and experiences, even if they seem trivial.

Step 9. Regular Check-Ins:

- Aim to journal regularly. It could be daily, weekly, or whenever you feel the need to express yourself.

Step 10. Reflect on Growth:

- Look back on your entries to see how you've grown and overcome challenges.

Remember, your journal is a personal space for self-reflection and growth. I hope you enjoy the process of discovering more about yourself during this transformative journey!

Chapter 7

Your Body, Your Choices

So, I got the gig to show around this new kid, Alex, who's gender fluid. At first, I was a bit clueless about what that meant. But I did some digging, and now I'm here to drop some knowledge bombs about gender identity, sexual orientation, and the LGBTQ+ world.

Gender Identity Basics

Alright, let's start simple. Gender identity is all about how you feel inside, like whether you see yourself as a boy, girl, both, neither, or something totally unique. And guess what? Loads of kids and teens, just like us, are figuring this stuff out and trying out different ways to express themselves.

Now, there's a term called "cisgender." That's when your gender matches what people assumed based on your birth parts. Like, if you were born with certain bits and you feel like they're you, you're cisgender. But hey, there's a whole rainbow of identities out there!

Some folks identify as "transgender." That means their gender doesn't line up with what they were assigned at birth. Others might call themselves "nonbinary," "gender fluid," "agender," or use words that fit them best. It's all about being true to yourself, no matter where you land on the gender spectrum.

Expressing Our Gender

So, how do we show the world our gender? It's all about the details! Names, pronouns, clothes, hairstyle, even our voice—these are the tools we use to let everyone know who we are. I mean, think about it; from when we were tiny tots, we've been shouting to the world, "This is me!"

But here's the deal: Trying out different ways to express your gender is totally normal when you're growing up. It doesn't automatically mean you're trans or exploring other genders. It's like trying on outfits until you find the one that makes you feel like a rockstar.

Gender Dysphoria

Now, let's talk about "gender dysphoria." It's when someone feels super upset because their gender identity doesn't match what they were assigned at birth. But not all trans or gender-diverse peeps go through this – some are perfectly cool with who they are.

The most important thing, my friends, is to show love and support to anyone who's exploring their gender identity or sexual orientation. Be a good friend, have those open chats, and be there to lift them up! Together, we can create a world where everyone's free to be their amazing selves.

The Fourth Wave of Feminism

Let's talk about something super important: the Fourth Wave of feminism. It's like the newest update in the fight for gender equality, and it's kind of a big deal. So, let's break it down in a way that makes sense for us (Abrahams, 2017).

Equality? Not quite yet: Some people used to think that we already had gender equality. I mean, laws were put in place to give us equal rights, right? But here's the kicker: Equality in the books doesn't always mean equality in real life. We still face things like the gender pay gap, where women are paid less for the same work as men. It's like getting the short end of the stick just because of your gender. Not cool!

Everyday sexism: Enter the Everyday Sexism Project. It's like this awesome online movement where people share their experiences of sexism and discrimination. It's not about a one-time thing; it's about showing that these issues happen daily. From being catcalled on the street to facing workplace discrimination, it's all part of the fight for gender equality.

Intersectionality: Fourth-wave feminism is all about being inclusive. It's not just about women – it's about supporting everyone, regardless of their gender or background. We're all in this together, and everyone's voice matters. Some people face more challenges than others, and we need to recognize that.

No more "One size fits all": The cool thing about this wave is that it's not a one-size-fits-all kind of deal. We're all different, and our experiences are unique. Some feminists say it's about choice – we should be free to choose what we want to do without judgment or barriers. Whether you want to be a CEO, a stay-at-home parent, or anything in between, it's all good!

Let's make waves: The Fourth Wave of feminism isn't just one thing – it's a bunch of voices, opinions, and ideas coming together. We're all part of this movement, and it's a powerful force for change. It's not always pretty or comfortable, but it's making a difference.

So, whether you're passionate about gender equality, fighting everyday sexism, or just being your awesome self, you're part of this amazing wave of feminism. We're rewriting the rules and making the world a better place for everyone. Go, team!

Your Body, Your Choice

I guess the decision to get sexually active is a highly personal one, and as long as it is consensual and safe, and both partners are totally comfortable with their decision to level up their relationship, it shouldn't be a problem. But just to make sure that you are ready to swipe that V-card, I suggest talking to a trusted grown-up about your decision first.

There are other factors to consider when making decisions about sex and sexuality. Then, there are the basics about sexual orientation and gender fluidity. The scariest part about taking the plunge and getting sexually active is the risks involved. I'm talking about teen pregnancy, STIs, and all sorts of risks. I must say that I am in no hurry to start thinking about all of that stuff, but I know of loads of teens my age who are comfortably practicing safe sex, too.

Discovering Dating During the Teenage Years

Ugh, the whole dating scene can be a total rollercoaster, right? Teen hormones are like, "Hello, crush city!" Some of us are psyched about it. Others? Not so much. Learning to socialize outside the fam is a big deal, though, and finding those real connections is key.

For the shy peeps, group dates are a total lifesaver – no one-on-one pressure, phew! Now, for the brave souls, some might wanna dip their toes into the dating pool. But, hold up, those hormones don't have to run the show.

So, here's the scoop: Look for people who vibe with your interests. Yeah, physical attraction is a thing, but having common hobbies makes for way better dates. Clubs, sports, you name it – that's where you find the real connections (Teenage Hormones & Sexuality, 2012). And here's a tip: Focus on the other person. It helps beat those jitters.

And okay, Grace and I aren't diving into this dating drama just yet, but we've seen friends take the plunge. It's not just butterflies and rainbows – emotions can get messy.

Diversity in Relationships

When it comes to dealing with diversity in a teen relationship, here are some valuable insights:

- **Open and respectful communication:** The foundation of any healthy relationship is communication. Encourage open, honest, and respectful conversations with your partner. Listen to their perspective and share yours. Understanding each other's backgrounds and experiences can lead to a deeper connection.

- **Embrace differences:** Diversity in a relationship can lead to a broader worldview. Instead of seeing differences as obstacles, consider them as opportunities for personal growth. Embrace the chance to learn from one another and expand your horizons.

- **Celebrate individuality:** In a diverse relationship, it's essential to celebrate each other's unique qualities. Recognize the beauty in the things that make you both different and the aspects that bind you together. This not only strengthens your bond but also fosters a sense of acceptance.

- **Address challenges together:** No relationship is without its challenges, but dealing with diversity may introduce unique obstacles. Whether it's differences in cultural backgrounds, values, or beliefs, address these challenges as a team. Work together to find solutions and compromises that respect both partners' needs.

- **Seek support when needed:** Sometimes, it can be beneficial to seek support from trusted adults or professionals, like counselors or therapists, when navigating complex issues related to diversity. They can offer guidance and strategies to help you both understand and appreciate each other better.

- **Be respectful and inclusive:** Respect for each other's backgrounds and experiences is the cornerstone of a healthy, diverse relationship. Avoid making assumptions, stereotyping, or being judgmental. Embrace inclusivity and celebrate the love that transcends differences.

Remember, diversity in a relationship is a strength, not a weakness. It's an opportunity to learn, grow, and create a deeper connection with your partner. By fostering open communication, respect, and acceptance, you can build a strong and resilient bond that thrives on the beautiful tapestry of human diversity.

Toxic Relationships

We all know being a teenager is already a rollercoaster of emotions, so it's crucial to make sure those emotions aren't being messed with in a toxic relationship. It is vital that we are able to protect our friends by being able to pick up on the red flags – tell-tale signs they are in a toxic relationship (*How to Spot Signs of a Toxic Teen Relationship - Troubled Teens*, 2022).

Warning Signs

But here's the deal, folks. Love can sometimes make us ignore signs of an unhealthy relationship. And Aunt Moira made it crystal clear that these are the warning signs that your relationship might be toxic:

- **Jealousy and possessiveness:** Your partner is overly jealous, possessive, or controlling. If they're isolating you from friends and family, constantly texting, or checking your phone, it's a red flag.

- **Pressure:** If your partner is pressuring you to have sex and not respecting your reasons for saying no, that's a huge problem.

- **Control and threats:** Your partner tries to control you through bullying or threats of self-harm if you end the relationship.

- **Disregarding protection:** They don't respect your desire to use condoms or birth control. Safety should always be a priority.

- **Insecurity and low self-esteem:** One major sign that something's not right is when your friend or you start feeling super insecure or have low self-esteem. If you or your friend suddenly doubts your awesomeness, it's time to take a closer look.

- **A decision-making zombie:** You know your friend's a total decision-making boss. But when she's in a toxic relationship, she might suddenly turn into a decision-making zombie. She lets her partner call all the shots, and that's just not like her.

- **Withdrawal from the squad:** Your bestie used to be all about squad goals, but now she's MIA from all your hangouts. If she's ditching the squad and her usual peeps for her partner, that's a big ol' red flag.

- **Partner surveillance:** When her partner starts acting like a round-the-clock private investigator, it's a problem. If they're constantly checking up on her, wanting to know where she is, who she's with, and why she hasn't texted back in two seconds, Houston, we've got an issue.

- **Phone separation anxiety:** A phone is a phone, right? Nope, not in a toxic relationship. If your friend gets super anxious when she can't stay connected to her partner via her phone, that's a sign that things might be going south.

Now, here's the deal: You can't always be the superhero that saves your friend from a toxic relationship. They often need to figure it out on their own. But you can be their sidekick, dropping some knowledge along the way (*How to Spot Signs of a Toxic Teen Relationship-Troubled Teens*, 2022).

- **Know the fine line:** Sometimes, there's a fine line between a caring partner and a controlling one. In the beginning, it might all seem sweet and protective. But if that protection turns into control, it's a red alert.

- **Protective versus possessive:** A protective boyfriend looks out for you when you need it, respects your decisions, and wants you to be safe. That's like, superhero material. But when it turns possessive, it's a whole different story. He might not want you hanging with certain friends or doing things you love without him. No bueno.

- **Bad vibes wrapped in love:** Toxic relationships often start with these sneaky controlling behaviors that seem like they're coming from a place of love. They try to make you feel guilty for spending time with your family or doing things that make you happy. That's not love; that's manipulation.

- **It's not your fault:** Remember, it's never your friend's fault if she's in a toxic relationship. These manipulative tactics can make her feel like it's all her fault, but it's not. Nobody deserves that kind of treatment (*How to Spot Signs of a Toxic Teen Relationship - Troubled Teens*, 2022).

- **Getting help:** If you suspect your friend is in a toxic relationship, reach out to a trusted adult, counselor, or teacher. They can offer guidance and support. If you're in one yourself, open up to someone who can help, like a parent or close friend (*How to Spot Signs of a Toxic Teen Relationship - Troubled Teens*, 2022).

Remember, you're not alone, and there are resources out there to help teens in toxic relationships. Your safety and happiness should always come first.

Bouncing Back From a Toxic Relationship

Getting down to business, let's rip off the band-aid and talk about how to recover from a toxic relationship. You know, the kind that makes you want to run faster than a caffeinated squirrel? Yep, those (Rahman, LCSW, 2022).

- **Step 1. Recognize it's toxic:** First things first, you gotta recognize that your relationship is about as toxic as a glow-in-the-dark fish in a neon pond. If you've been feeling sad, anxious, or like a whole piece of you is missing, it's time to wave goodbye to those toxic vibes.

- **Step 2. Cut off all contact:** Chop, chop! Snip, snip! Sayonara, toxic ex. Seriously, cut off all contact. Block 'em on social media, delete their number, and maybe even consider moving to a remote island without Wi-Fi. Okay, maybe not the last one, but you get the idea.

- **Step 3. Rally the troops:** Your friends and family are your army of emotional superheroes. Reach out to them, and let them know you're going through a breakup battle. They'll have your back, and they'll remind you why you're awesome.

- **Step 4. Find your self-worth:** Toxic relationships often make you feel like a crumpled piece of paper. But guess what? You're a work of art, baby! Start believing that you deserve better. Positive affirmations are your new BFFs.

- **Step 5. Seek professional help:** Therapists aren't just for the movies. Talking to a therapist can be super helpful in this tough time. They'll help you cope, rebuild your self-esteem, and create a game plan for moving forward.

- **Step 6. Keep a journal:** Grab a notebook and pour your heart out. Write down your feelings, even if it feels like a rollercoaster of emotions. It might seem tough at first, but it's like an emotional detox. You'll feel better in the long run.

- **Step 7. Plan your escape:** Make a plan to escape the toxic tornado. Think about your financial independence, where you'll live, and what possessions you'll take with you. It's like plotting a superhero mission – you got this!

- **Step 8. Surround yourself with positivity:** Hang out with people who make you feel like sunshine on a cloudy day. Treat yourself to your fave meal, dance like nobody's watching, and just do stuff that makes your heart sing.

- **Step 9. Express your feelings:** When you're ready, have a heart-to-heart with your toxic ex. Express your feelings honestly but without pointing fingers. It's all about saying, "This is how you made me feel," not "You made me feel this way."

- **Step 10. Stick to your decision:** It's normal to miss the good times, but remember why you left in the first place. Stay strong, lean on your support squad, and remind yourself that you deserve a relationship that lifts you up, not drags you down.

- **Step 11. Stay firm and keep moving forward:** Don't look back; you're not going that way! Stay firm with your decision, and keep marching forward. Your future is brighter without toxic shadows.

Healthy Decision-Making About Sex

Aunt Moira and I just had the most eye-opening, heart-to-heart chat about making healthy decisions when it comes to sex as a teen. Yeah, you heard it right – the "S" word. But don't worry, it's all about keeping you informed and empowered (*For Teens: How to Make Healthy Decisions about Sex*, 2019).

Consent and Clarity of Thought

So, before we dive into the juicy bits, here are some important reminders Aunt Moira shared with me: No one – and I mean NO ONE – should ever be forced or pressured into having sex. It's essential to remember that, and if it ever happens to you or someone you know, reach out to a trusted adult for help, and never blame yourself. There's medical and counseling support available for situations like that.

Now, let's talk about a biggie: **alcohol and drugs**. Aunt Moira emphasized how these substances can seriously mess with your decision-making when it comes to sex. Trust me, you don't want to end up in a situation where you're doing something you didn't intend to because you're under the influence. It's just not worth it.

Are You Ready for Sex?

Sex is a game-changer, my friends. It can affect your life and your relationships in ways you might not even realize. Aunt Moira stressed that waiting until you're genuinely ready is crucial. And guess what? The "right time" is different for everyone. Some teens might want to wait until they're adults, married, or just feel their relationship is ready to take that step.

Here are some signs that your relationship might be ready for the next level:

- **Trust and honesty:** You can be completely honest with your partner, and they can be honest with you. Open communication is key!

- **Talking about the nitty-gritty**: You can discuss challenging topics like feelings, other relationships, sexually transmitted infections (STIs), condoms, or pregnancy prevention without hesitation.

- **Responsibility:** You're both responsible individuals who are willing to protect yourselves and your partner against STIs and unwanted pregnancy using condoms and birth control.

- **Respect:** You respect your partner's decisions, whether they want to wait or are comfortable moving forward.

- **Privacy:** You have a private and safe space where you can share this intimate moment.

Why Wait?

But why wait to have sex? Well, there's a lot to think about, folks. Sex can lead to pregnancy, and you have to be prepared for that. It comes with tough decisions like becoming a teen parent, considering adoption, or ending a pregnancy. Those are major life choices with significant effects on your health, finances, education, relationships, and family.

Sex also comes with health risks, and Aunt Moira didn't sugarcoat it. There are plenty of infections that can be spread during sex, including chlamydia, gonorrhea, herpes, HIV (that's the virus causing AIDS), human papillomavirus (HPV), and syphilis. Some are treatable, but others can stick around for a lifetime.

And let's not forget the emotional side of things. You might feel sad or angry if you're pressured into sex when you're not ready. Or, if you do decide to have sex, there's the risk of your partner breaking up with you or sharing intimate details with others. It can be a rollercoaster of emotions.

Protection

Now, the big question: How can you protect yourself from getting an STI? Well, the best way is to use a barrier method, like a condom or dental dam, every single time you have sex—no exceptions. Aunt Moira emphasized the importance of regular medical checkups and getting the HPV vaccine to stay healthy.

Remember, you can't always tell if someone has an STI just by looking at them or talking to them. Many STIs don't cause symptoms, so it's better to be safe than sorry.

Now, let's chat about barrier protection, specifically condoms. Both external (male) and internal (female) condoms have a very high chance of preventing pregnancy – but they have to be used correctly every single time.

Condoms

Here's what you need to know about condoms:

- Never use both external and internal condoms simultaneously; they might tear.

- Follow the instructions on the package carefully.

- Check the expiration date – no expired condoms, please!

- Don't store them in hot or damaged places, like the glove compartment of your car or wallet.

Birth Control

And if you're wondering about other forms of birth control, Aunt Moira had the lowdown. The most effective ones are the contraceptive implant, intrauterine devices (IUDs), and the contraceptive injection. These options are highly effective when used as prescribed and can prevent pregnancy for several years.

Then there are birth control pills, patches, and rings, which contain hormones and are very effective when used correctly. But remember, consistency is key here.

Alternative Ways to Express Love

My folks are kinda into old-school music. I'm talking about music from Gramp's time. They were singing an oldie called "50 Ways to Leave Your Lover." That song kinda stuck in my head, even though it ain't my jam. Later that day, my girls Grace and Amelia and I were just chillin', sippin' on our frappuccinos and talkin' about all the awesome ways we can show love without, you know, getting all down and dirty.

So, I told them about the song and thought we could do a remix called "50 Ways to Love Your Lover." We came up with this epic list of 15 ways to make that special someone feel totally loved. Check it out (*GIO*, n.d.)! You know that bae loves you when they can:

- **Support and appreciate you:** 'Cause you're awesome just the way you are.

- **Give you a cuddle:** Hugs are like free therapy, right?

- **Look after you when you're ill:** Even if it means pretending to be a nurse.

- **Pay you lots of compliments:** "You're, like, the most amazing human ever!"

- **Make you a present:** Handmade stuff rules!

- **Respect you for who you are:** No judgment zone, baby.

- **Take you out for dinner or cook for you:** Who can resist a home-cooked meal?

- **Send you a romantic text message:** Emoji hearts for days!

- **Be honest with you:** No lies, just truth bombs.

- **Surprise you:** 'Cause life's better with a little mystery.

- **Give you your own space:** Sometimes you just need a breather.

- **Be faithful to you/not cheat on you:** Loyalty is sexy.

- **Be understanding:** "I totally get you, babe."

- **Respect your decisions:** Even if it's choosing pineapple on pizza.

- **Always think about how you feel:** Mind-reading skills are on point.

So there you have it! Fifteen epic ways to show someone you're head over heels in love without takin' it to the next level. Love is all about the little things, right? I think it is uber romantic to express love with these kinda gestures.

Online Dating

Do you know what's becoming totally normal these days? Taking your dating game online! Thanks to our trusty smartphones, online dating is as common as scrolling through your favorite social media app. It's all about swiping left and right, chatting, and maybe even finding someone special. So, let's dive into some tips to keep you safe in the world of online dating (Rutledge, 2022).

Here Are a Few Online Dating Tips

- **Age-appropriate platforms:** Use dating apps designed for teens. They're a safer choice.

- **Always inform a trusted adult:** Let someone you trust know about your online dating intentions.

- **Avoid sharing personal info:** Don't give out your last name, school, or home address. Use a fake name for extra privacy.

- **Meet in public:** If you decide to meet someone you've talked to online, do it in a public place where there are other people around.

- **Trust your instincts:** If something feels off about the person you're talking to, trust your gut and back away.

- **Avoid explicit content:** Don't share or ask for explicit photos or messages. It's not cool, and it can get you into trouble.

- **Respect boundaries:** Respect the other person's boundaries and expect them to respect yours.

- **Privacy settings:** Learn how to set privacy features on your dating app to control who can contact you.

- **Verify identity:** Make sure the person you're talking to is who they say they are. Video calls can help with this.

So, remember, online dating is an adventure, kinda like leveling up in your favorite video game. As long as you stay safe and make good choices, you can enjoy the journey with confidence and excitement. Happy dating!

Activity: Online Safety Quiz

Let's put your online safety knowledge to the test! This quiz will help you gauge your awareness and caution when it comes to using dating apps and social media. Remember, the more informed you are, the better equipped you'll be to make safe choices online. So, grab a piece of paper or your device and jot down your answers. Don't worry; we'll provide the answers at the end!

Question 1: True or False?

Sexting is a fun and harmless way to flirt with someone you like online.

Question 2: Multiple Choice

What should you do if someone you've been chatting with online requests explicit photos from you?

a) Send the photos

b) Ignore the request

c) Report the person to the app or website

d) Tell your friends about it

Question 3: True or False?

Online relationships are not as real as in-person ones.

Question 4: Multiple Choice

Which of the following is an important step to take before meeting someone in person whom you've met online?

a) Share your exact location with them

b) Tell a trusted friend or family member about the meeting

c) Keep the meeting a secret

d) Meet them at a secluded place

Question 5: True or False?

Teens should keep their online dating activities secret from their parents or guardians.

Question 6: Multiple Choice

What is one thing you should do when dealing with online bullying or harassment?

a) Respond with insults

b) Block the person

c) Share the messages with everyone

d) Keep it to yourself

Question 7: True or False?

It's essential to discuss your online dating experiences and concerns with a trusted adult.

Question 8: Multiple Choice

What's the best way to avoid falling for an online scam?

a) Share personal information with strangers

b) Always send money to someone you've never met

c) Be cautious and skeptical about requests for money or personal information

d) Share your financial details without any hesitation

Question 9: True or False?

It's okay to meet someone you've been talking to online without telling anyone about it.

Question 10: Multiple Choice

When creating an online dating profile, it's best to:

a) Use your full name and birthdate

b) Use a fake name to protect your identity

c) Share limited personal information

d) Include personal contact information like your phone number

Answers:

1: False, 2: c, 3: False, 4: b, 5: False, 6: b, 7: True, 8: c, 9: False, 10: c

How did you do? Count up your correct answers and see how well you scored. Remember, staying safe online is about making informed choices and being cautious. Share this quiz with your friends and family so they can test their online safety knowledge, too!

Chapter 8

BASIC SURVIVAL SKILLS

During one of Ms. Bennet's classes, she had us watch a reality TV show where teens were thrown into the deep end. They had to handle households, including budgeting, buying, cooking, cleaning, taking care of younger siblings, and maintaining the house. All this had to be done on a tight budget while also holding down a summer job.

Honestly, I'd probably quit in the first episode or get kicked off the show. I'm just not prepared for life's challenges. But it's not too late to learn.

Let's dive into Life Skills 101!

Budgeting and Money Smarts

First things first – if you're gonna manage a household or just your own life, you need a budget. Let's talk money because no one wants to be an adult and be broke, right?

- **Needs vs. wants:** Needs are the must-haves for survival, like food and a place to live. Wants are like the extra toppings on your pizza – nice but not essential. Do you really need that shiny new gadget?

- **Live below your means:** Don't splurge on everything. Living below your means is like having a secret stash of money for emergencies. Cooking at home can save you cash, and having roommates can be fun if you're in college or starting out after high school.

- **Set savings goals:** Saving might not sound exciting, but it's like leveling up in a video game. Set goals, break them into smaller chunks, and you're on your way to owning that epic gaming console or dream vacation.

- **Don't wait to invest:** The sooner you start investing, the more your money can grow. Think of it like planting seeds for a money tree, but with stocks or something. Time is your best friend in investing.

- **Build skills:** You can't survive on your allowance forever, right? Learning skills like cooking, budgeting, and laundry may not be thrilling, but they'll save you tons when you're on your own. Plus, who doesn't want to be a kitchen wizard?

- **Multiple income streams:** Think side hustles, online gigs, or helping your neighbors. Having more than one way to earn money is like having extra lives in a video game. You'll be less stressed if one income source takes a hit.

- **Gross pay vs. net pay:** That paycheck is great, but then taxes swoop in like a villain in a superhero movie. What you see on your paycheck isn't all yours. Taxes take their share.

- **Good vs. bad debt:** Student loans for college? Sometimes, they're a good investment because they can lead to better opportunities. But maxed-out credit cards? That's like inviting chaos to your party.

- **Start building credit:** Building credit is like unlocking new levels in a game. It helps you get better deals on things like cars and apartments when you're ready. Get a credit card, use it wisely, and watch your credit score soar.

- **Get creative about building wealth:** The world's your playground, and there are countless ways to make money. Starting a business, getting creative with investments, or any other bold idea—go for it! Being inventive with your finances can lead to incredible rewards.

- **Improve your financial literacy:** Learning about money isn't a one-time deal. Keep leveling up your money knowledge. Take courses, read books, or chat with experienced adults who've mastered the art of adulting.

Creating a Budget

As a teen, making a budget is about managing your money and setting yourself up for financial success. Let's break it down into five easy steps.

Step 1. Figure out your income: Know how much money you make each month, not just the occasional gifts. If you're paid every two weeks, divide that amount by two for your weekly budgeting.

Step 2. Track your expenses: Keep tabs on every penny you spend for at least a week or better yet, a month. Use a notebook, a spreadsheet, or a budgeting app. It's like detective work for your spending habits. Here are a few apps you can check out (Williams, 2019):

- **Greenlight:** This app is like a debit card with parental controls. It allows us and our parents to monitor our spending. We can also set up savings goals.

- **FamZoo:** FamZoo is a family finance app. It can help us manage our allowance and chores. Plus, it comes with prepaid cards and no overdraft fees.

- **Plan'it Prom:** If we're planning to go to prom, this app helps with budgeting and countdowns.

- **BusyKid:** This app is designed to teach kids how to earn, save, spend, and invest money. We can earn money for doing chores and even get bonuses for extra tasks.

- **Tip Yourself:** Tip Yourself is a habit-building app. It encourages us to save money for different accomplishments, like getting paid or achieving goals.

- **Mint:** Mint is a popular app for managing money. It's great for tracking spending and setting budgets. It can give us reminders if we're overspending.

These apps make managing money more fun and teach us important financial skills. It's like having a financial coach right on our phones!

Step 3. Identify your spending: Sort your spending into needs (like school stuff) and wants (like gaming). Break down wants into categories, like hobbies or social outings.

Step 4. Subtract necessities from earnings: Add up your necessary expenses and subtract them from your income. This leaves you with what you have for fun stuff and saving. If you're spending more than you earn, it's time to cut back on non-necessities.

Step 5. Create savings goals: Start saving for emergencies and future goals. Whether it's a dream apartment, new kicks, or concert tickets, saving is the way to go. I like following the 50/30/20 rule in which half my money goes toward my needs, 30% goes toward my wants, and I save 20% of my income.

Budgeting doesn't have to be boring; it's about taking control of your money game. Happy budgeting, folks!

What's Cookin'?

Let's keep it real, fam. In the kitchen, besides salads and sandwiches, my culinary skills are close to zero. But after watching a teen reality show, I realized cooking is a survival skill – we all gotta eat, right? So, I got inspired and decided to up my kitchen game. If you're ready for some teen chef action, grab your knives, and let's cook!

As modern teens, we're super busy. Meals need to be simple, nutritious, and tasty. Try a meal planning schedule to do your grocery shopping for the week in one go and make daily meal prep easier.

Meal Planning

Life is crazy, and we gotta master meal planning. Trust me, it's not that hard, and it'll save you money and hunger later on. Here's how to meal plan like a boss (Hideout, 2020)!

- **Get involved:** Start by helping plan meals at home. Suggest your favorite dishes. It's not rocket science, and it's a useful skill.

- **Keep it simple:** Don't stress. Start with easy meals like spaghetti, tacos, grilled cheese with soup, or a simple casserole. The goal is to feel confident, not overwhelmed.

- **Create favorites:** With endless online recipes, make a list of your go-to meals. Keep it handy for those "What's for dinner?" moments. You can also try teen-friendly meal kit services for simplicity.

- **Check your kitchen:** Before you shop, see what's in your fridge and pantry. Use up leftovers and forgotten ingredients. Get creative!

- **Leftovers are great:** Plan a leftover night. It's like a mini feast without cooking. Less food wasted, more money saved, and a night off from cooking.

- **Challenge yourself:** Teen challenges are fun! Stick to your meal plan for a week, then a month, and beyond. Slip up? No worries; just keep going. Challenge your friends, too, and earn points for every planned meal you nail!

Meal planning is a teen superpower. It's about independence, saving cash, and satisfying your hunger. Give it a shot, and you might become a household chef extraordinaire!

Cooking Techniques and Methods

I got to read more about the dos and don'ts in the kitchen and learned some nifty stuff (Stinger, 2021). Check it out.

- **Cooking spray on nonstick pans? Hard pass:** Seriously, guys, resist the urge to blast that cooking spray on nonstick pans. It's like kryptonite for them. Stick to medium heat, and your food won't stage a sticky rebellion. Oh, and don't even think about metal utensils – those pans are sensitive souls.

- **The proof is in the tasting:** Imagine pouring your heart into cooking, only to realize your ingredients are past their prime. Taste as you go, folks. And check those expiration dates – no one wants a rendezvous with spoiled eggs.

- **Wash those meat hooks:** Raw meat can be sneaky with its bacteria buddies. After wrestling with the meat, wash your hands like you're getting ready to perform surgery. No bacteria escape artists allowed! Ensure that you wash the chopping board and knives thoroughly before using them for veggies or something else.

- **Kitchen couture:** Cooking can get messy – like, "Oops, I dropped the tomato sauce on my white shirt" messy. Rock an apron; it's like a superhero cape for your clothes.

- **The right stuff:** Before you start your culinary masterpiece, make sure you've got everything and the right stuff. Nobody wants a mid-cooking grocery store dash. Trust me; it's not a fun race.

- **Substitutes are a game-changer:** Allergies or dietary preferences? No worries. Look for smart swaps that actually work. I'm talking about stuff like almond milk, brown rice noodles, and gluten-free flour. Avoid corn noodles; they're basically glue disguised as pasta.

- **Cool burns off:** Burns need to be cooled. Try placing the burned area gently under cool running water for about 10 to 20 minutes.

- **Recipe rules are real:** Some recipes are like secret codes – every step matters. Follow 'em like your life depends on it. Read the recipe carefully, and if you're confused, Google's your best friend.

- **Avoid messy pileups:** Cooking's fun, but it's also a mess-making machine. Try cleaning up as you cook. It's a bit annoying at first, but trust me, it's worth it. Start small, tidy up ingredients, and work your way to dishes.

- **Simplicity equals deliciousness:** You don't need to be a culinary wizard to create epic meals. Love and passion for food are what truly matter. Even a bowl of chili can be magical when made with heart. So, cook with love, and your food will speak volumes!

Remember, cooking is like a delicious adventure, and the best part? You get to eat the treasure at the end. Happy cooking, champs!

Emily's Top Go-To Recipes for Quick and Easy Meals

As you know, my folks are uber busy, and they grab meals on the go. Hannah and I have a few go-to hunger-busters that work for us. I thought I'd share them with my peeps. Ready to whip up some delicious and fuss-free meals? Let's get cooking with these recipes that even kitchen rookies can conquer (Sally, 2021). No fancy chef hats required!

Pizza bagel: It's pizza, but easier! Grab a sliced bagel or some French bread. Top it with pizza sauce, cheese, and your favorite toppings. Stick it under the broiler or in the toaster oven. Voila! You've got a homemade pizza bagel.

Frozen pasta: Boil frozen tortellini or ravioli and serve with red sauce from a jar or a drizzle of olive oil and parmesan cheese. Quick, easy, and a pasta lover's dream!

Dinner leftovers: Got some dinner leftovers? Pop them into single-portion glass containers. Heat 'em up in the microwave for lunch the next day. Leftovers just got cool.

Nachos: Top corn tortilla chips with beans and cheese, then zap 'em in the microwave. Add salsa, tomatoes, or avocado for extra flavor. Nacho ordinary lunch!

Scrambled egg muffins: Whisk up some eggs with your favorite protein and veggies, bake 'em in muffin cups, and store them for later. Easy breakfast-for-lunch vibes.

Mac and cheese: No judgment here – box mac and cheese is a winner. Make it healthier with a side salad or mixed veggies. Cheesy goodness!

Pesto pasta: Try out this Lunchbox Pesto Tortellini with kale, walnuts, and spinach. Boil up your pasta; blanch or steam your greens; mix with a generous dose of your fave pesto; add walnuts. Toss in cherry tomatoes for a fresh twist. Make it ahead and refrigerate or freeze for later.

Soup or chili: Warm up with a hearty soup or chili. Look for options with beans or meat for protein and veggies. Perfect for a chilly day.

Practical Life Skills – Chores and Laundry

I know that parents make it seem like it's the easiest thing in the world to keep the house running smoothly. In that reality show called, "Teenwork Makes the Dream Work," we got to see just what skills are involved in the day-to-day operations of a household. It was quite an eye-opener!

Household Chores

I'm sure, like me, you love to live in a clean and clutter-free space without the hassle of doing any of the chores it takes to get the house looking neat (Donely, 2020).

I've got some epic insider tips to help you conquer those pesky household chores and keep your parents' sanity intact. Buckle up because we're about to turn cleaning into a total breeze.

- **Chores versus maintenance – know the difference:** So, there's something we need to hash out from the get-go: the distinction between "chores" and "maintenance." Chores are those big cleaning missions that involve rubber gloves, scrubbing, and vacuuming. It's like a weekly deep cleanse for your home. Maintenance, on the other hand, is what you do on the daily. They're the little things you do to put things back and keep your space clean, like hanging up your towel after a shower, tossing dirty clothes in the hamper, or loading your cereal bowl into the dishwasher, for instance. Maintenance is about keeping things tidy without breaking a sweat.

- **Shift your mindset:** I'm not asking you to be perfect because, trust me, I'm far from it! But here's the deal, peeps – while you might someday have the moolah to hire a cleaning crew for your "chores" (dream big, right?), you'll definitely have to tackle "daily maintenance" for the rest of your life. So, it's essential to master this skill now.

- **Thursday cleaning rocks!:** Now, here's a game-changer: clean on a Thursday. Why Thursday, you ask? Well, everyone still has some juice left in the tank, and you head into the weekend with a squeaky-clean home. Plus, by Friday, you're toast.

Get some pizza on the way home, and everyone dives in together for 1-2 hours. Blast some tunes, set a timer, and tackle those tasks. It's like a cleaning party! If conflicts pop up, figure it out because Thursday is your powerhouse day.

Laundry Basics

I'm about to spill the beans on how to conquer the mysterious world of laundry. Yeah, I know it might not sound like the most exciting topic, but trust me, it's a life skill you're gonna need when you're out there on your own, whether you're heading off to college, moving into your own place, or just wanna impress your parents with your newfound laundry prowess (Bostwick, 2016).

- **Tags:** First things first, let's talk about those little tags on your clothes. You know, those symbols that seem like a secret code? Well, they're actually super helpful. They tell you things like whether your clothes can handle the washing machine, what water temperature to use, and whether it's okay to toss them in the dryer. So, before you even buy that cute new outfit, take a peek at the tag and make sure you're down with its laundry requirements.

- **Laundry care:** Now, let's get down to the nitty-gritty of laundry care, starting with stain prevention. Keep an eye out for any stains while you're wearing your clothes. If you spill something, don't wait – treat that stain ASAP. Empty your pockets, close zippers, and make sure everything is buttoned up. Oh, and don't forget to tie those strings and sashes loosely. Nobody wants a tangled mess in the laundry.

- **Detergents:** Before you even start, make sure you've got the essentials: laundry detergent, fabric softener, bleach, and nonchlorine bleach. It's like assembling your superhero squad for laundry day.

- **Sorting:** Now, let's talk sorting. Most of the time, I'm too lazy to separate whites from darks, but for new stuff, it's a must. You don't want that cute white shirt turning into a pink disaster, right? Also, keep an eye out for lint-givers and lint-takers. Terry cloth, towels, and corduroy should never dance together in the same load. Watch out for color bleeding. Some clothes are like the rebels of the laundry world and bleed their colors onto others. Sorting and washing separately is your best defense. And if it does happen, don't toss those items in the dryer. Pre-treat and rewash, or let the sun work its magic.

- **Stains:** Speaking of stains, get yourself a stain pre-treater or use baby wipes for those little buggers.

- **Load size:** Now, let's talk load size. Don't go overboard and stuff the washer like a Thanksgiving turkey. Use the right load size for the amount of laundry you've got. Also, measure your detergent and fabric softener. More is not better in this case. And if you're using bleach, mix it with water before adding your clothes. Safety first!

- **Drying:** Once the washer's done its thing, it's time to decide how to dry your clothes. I'm all for the eco-friendly vibe, so if you can, hang 'em outside. But if it's a blizzard or raining outside, the dryer is your best buddy. Just remember to shake those clothes out before tossing them in. And always check for stains before drying; once they're dry, they're like permanent tattoos.

  ○ Clean that lint filter after every use. Seriously, it's a fire hazard and slows down your drying time. Every few months, give the dryer a little space and check the exhaust pipe for lint and cracks. Safety, peeps!

  ○ Taking your laundry out of the dryer pronto is key to avoiding wrinkles. Fold 'em as you go, and don't let that laundry pile up. Trust me; it's easier to put away one load at a time than tackle

Mount Laundry later.

- **Ironing:** Lastly, if you've got stuff that needs ironing, check the labels for ironing instructions. Some like it hot, some not so much. Now you're all set to tackle the laundry world like a pro!

Laundry may seem like a chore, but with a little know-how, you'll be the master of your laundry kingdom. It's all about those small victories in life, right? And knowing how to keep your clothes looking fresh is definitely one of 'em. So go forth and conquer the laundry room!

There you have it, folks! All the know-how teens need to survive no matter what – brought to you by your girl, Emily!

Activity: Financial Vision Board

Creating a financial vision board is a fun and creative way to set and visualize your short-, medium-, and long-term financial goals. It's a visual reminder of what you want to achieve and can help keep you motivated as you work toward your dreams.

Before you start, find a quiet and inspiring space to work on your vision board. Gather some old magazines, a board or canvas, colorful markers, stickers, and, most importantly, your financial goals.

Here's a template to get you started:

- **Section 1. Short-Term Goals (0-1 year):** For each short-term goal, add a picture or draw an image that represents your short-term goal, write a brief description of the goal, and specify when you aim to achieve this goal.

- **Section 2. Medium-Term Goals (1-5 years):** For each medium-term goal, add a picture or draw an image that represents your short-term goal, write a brief description of the goal, and specify when you aim to achieve this goal.

- **Section 3. Long-Term Goals (5+ years):** For each long-term goal, add a picture or draw an image that represents your short-term goal, write a brief description of the goal, and specify when you aim to achieve this goal.

- **Section 4. Affirmations:** Write down positive affirmations related to your financial goals. For example, "I am in control of my financial future" or "I am capable of achieving my goals."

- **Section 5. Signature:** Sign and date your financial vision board. This represents your commitment to working towards your financial dreams.

Remember, your financial vision board is a personal and creative expression of your goals. Feel free to get as creative as you like, and don't forget to revisit and update your vision board as you accomplish your goals and set new ones. Good luck on your financial journey!

Conclusion

Hey there, my fabulous fellow girls!

We've just graduated from the ultimate teenage survival boot camp, and let me tell you, we're walking away with the crown jewels of knowledge. We've mastered the art of navigating puberty's wild rollercoaster and expertly balanced everything from making the right career choices to juggling friends, family, and even budgets like total bosses. Developing a positive body image, improving our self-esteem, and navigating the internet got some traction here, too. Plus, we've whipped up dishes that won't send us running for the nearest takeout menu – culinary queens in the making!

Now, as we hurtle into the magnificent teen years and beyond, I want you to remember one thing: Each and every one of you is more fabulous than a glitter explosion at a unicorn convention. Life might throw curveballs at us like confetti, but guess what? We've got the skills to dodge, dip, dive, and dazzle through it all.

Here's the deal, my fierce friends: Stay true to your amazing selves, keep that thirst for knowledge burning, and flaunt your quirks like they're the hottest fashion accessories on the runway. Those dreams you're chasing? Chase 'em like they're the last piece of pizza at a sleepover – with determination and maybe a little bit of friendly competition. Don't ever be afraid to stand out in a world that often seems black-and-white when you've got the whole dang rainbow of possibilities inside you.

Life is one wild rollercoaster, and guess what? You're the fearless ride operator. Buckle up for the loops, corkscrews, and unexpected drops because you've got the steering wheel, and you're in control. Confidence is your superhero cape, and let me tell you, you're rocking it like the incredible superheroes you are.

So, go out there, conquer the world, and collect adventures like they're rare Pokémon cards – gotta catch 'em all! Embrace every quirky, wacky, and wonderful moment that life throws your way. You're not just living; you're thriving, sparkling, and owning your unique path.

With all the love, support, and girl power vibes in the universe,

Emily

I'D LOVE TO KNOW WHAT YOU THINK!

I hope you enjoyed reading *The Ultimate Teen Girl's Survival Guide.*

Writing this book was a labor of love, and I poured my heart into every chapter. As an independent author, your feedback means the world to me. I would be immensely grateful if you could please take a few moments to share your thoughts in a review.

Reviews are crucial in supporting authors like myself and helping other teens discover this book. I genuinely read every review and am excited to hear your thoughts.

Thank you!

Ready to share your thoughts? Scan one of the QR codes below:

Amazon US

Amazon Canada

Amazon UK

Amazon Australia

REFERENCES

5-Minute mindfulness body scan script for teens. (n.d.). https://www.mindfulschools.org/wp/wp-content/uploads/2019/02/Practice-Script-for-Teens-Body-Scan.pdf

8 Important car maintenance services teens and new drivers need to know. (n.d.). Www.travelers.com. https://www.travelers.com/resources/auto/maintenance/8-important-car-maintenance-services-teens-need-to-know

50 ways to show someone you love them, without having sex: Getting It On: GIO. (n.d.). www.gettingiton.org.uk. https://www.gettingiton.org.uk/50-ways-to-show-love

Abrahams, J. (2017, August 14). *Everything you wanted to know about fourth wave feminism—but were afraid to ask.* Dlv.prospect.gcpp.io. https://www.prospectmagazine.co.uk/culture/44809/everything-you-wanted-to-know-about-fourth-wave-feminismbut-were-afraid-to-ask

Akruti. (2017, January 6). *10 Common teenage girl problems and their solutions.* MomJunction. https://www.momjunction.com/articles/common-teenage-girls-problems-and-their-solutions_0078619/

Attend Career Fairs And Networking Events. (n.d.). www.kochind.com. https://www.kochind.com/careers/veterans/veterans-guide/attend-career-fairs-and-networking-events

Ayaad, F. (2021, January 29). *10 Non-Negotiable boundaries all strong women should have for their lives.* Thought Catalog. https://thoughtcatalog.com/farah-ayaad/2021/01/10-non-negotiable-boundaries-all-strong-women-should-have-for-their-lives/#:~:text=10

Being assertive and setting boundaries. (2020, May 13). Kids

Helpline. https://kidshelpline.com.au/teens/issues/being-assertive-and -setting-boundaries

Better Health. (2021, December 20). *Exercise and mental health*. Better Health Channel. https://www.betterhealth.vic.gov.au/health/healthyliv ing/exercise-and-mental-health

Better Health Channel. (2018, November 5). *Teenagers and sleep*. Vic.go v.au; Better health channel. https://www.betterhealth.vic.gov.au/health/ healthyliving/teenagers-and-sleep

biglifejournal.com. (2022, September 27). *15 Tips to build self esteem and confidence in teens*. Big Life Journal. https://biglifejournal.com/blogs/bl og/build-self-esteem-confidence-teens

Bleuet | girls first bra buying guide | find your perfect fit. (n.d.). Bleuet. Retrieved October 3, 2023, from https://bleuetgirl.com/pages/buying-y our-first-bra#:~:text=Whatever%20first%20bra%20style%20you

Bostwick, L. (2016, March 16). *Tips for teens- laundry how to*. Successful Homemakers. https://successfulhomemakers.com/tips-for-teens-laundr y-how-to/

Breehl, L., & Caban, O. (2022). *Physiology, puberty*. PubMed; StatPearls Publishing. https://www.ncbi.nlm.nih.gov/books/NBK534827/#:~:tex t=The%20rise%20in%20gonadotropins%20during

Buiano, M. (2022, May 18). *13 Super easy meals teens can make themselves*. Martha Stewart. https://www.marthastewart.com/1505773/13-super-e asy-meals-teens-can-make-themselves

Cafasso, J. (2018, September 18). *Synaptic pruning: Definition, early childhood, and more*. Healthline. https://www.healthline.com/health/sy naptic-pruning#:~:text=Synaptic%20pruning%20is%20a%20natural

Canadian Paediatric Society. (2008). Teens and sleep: Why you need it and how to get enough. *Paediatrics & Child Health, 13*(1), 69–70. https://www.ncbi.nlm.nih.gov/pmc/articles/PMC2528821/#:~ :text=Teens%20need%20more%20sleep%20because

Cherry, K. (2021, April 24). *Why self-esteem is important for success*. Very-well Mind. https://www.verywellmind.com/what-is-self-esteem-279586 8#:~:text=Why%20Self%2DEsteem%20Is%20Important

Chiu, B. (2020, March 8). *2020s Mark a new wave of feminist mobilization*. Forbes. https://www.forbes.com/sites/bonniechiu/2020/03/08/20 20s-mark-a-new-wave-of-feminist-mobilization/?sh=185e6e15485e

Chung, R. (2019, November 9). *Mental health and teens: Watch for danger signs.* HealthyChildren.org . https://www.healthychildren.org/English/ages-stages/teen/Pages/Men tal-Health-and-Teens-Watch-for-Danger-Signs.aspx

Cleeve, L. (2019, February 25). *Public transport tips for teens | RACV*. @RACV. https://www.racv.com.au/royalauto/transport/teens-public-t ransport.html

Clegg, B. (2017, January 12). *Five ways to rebel against society's body standards*. Recovery Warriors. https://recoverywarriors.com/reclaim-body-i mage/

Cleveland Clinic. (2023, May 1). *Adolescent Development | Cleveland Clinic*. Cleveland Clinic; Cleveland Clinic. https://my.clevelandclinic.o rg/health/articles/7060-adolescent-development

Cohen, M. (2021, October 15). *The best acne-fighting skincare routine, according to dermatologists*. Good Housekeeping. https://www.goodho usekeeping.com/beauty/anti-aging/a37856790/acne-skincare-routine/

Dealing with conflict – why it's worth it. (2018, July 18). Kids Helpline. https://kidshelpline.com.au/teens/issues/ways-deal-conflict

Digital Citizenship and Netiquette. (n.d.). Maryville Online. https://online.maryville.edu/online-bachelors-degrees/liberal-studies/dig ital-citizenship-and-netiquette-a-teachers-guide/#:~:text=The%20core%2 0netiquette%20rules%20are

Donely, C. (2020, January 22). *Get your teenager to do chores with humor and a checklist - empowered moms and kids*. www.empoweredmomsand kids.com. https://www.empoweredmomsandkids.com/get-your-teenage r-to-do-chores/

Dowshen, S. (2015). *Everything you wanted to know about puberty (for teens) - KidsHealth*. Kidshealth.org. https://kidshealth.org/en/teens/pub erty.html

Dutta, S. (2022, March 28). *Eating disorders and social media*. News

-Medical.net. https://www.news-medical.net/health/Eating-Disorders-a
nd-Social-Media.aspx

Ehmke, R. (2023, March 13). *How using social media affects teenagers.*
Child Mind Institute; Child Mind Institute. https://childmind.org/artic
le/how-using-social-media-affects-teenagers/

Fletcher, J. (2019, February 12). *4-7-8 breathing: How it works, benefits,
and uses.* www.medicalnewstoday.com. https://www.medicalnewstoday.
com/articles/324417#uses

For teens: How to make healthy decisions about sex. (2019). HealthyChildr
en.org. https://www.healthychildren.org/English/ages-stages/teen/datin
g-sex/Pages/Making-Healthy-Decisions-About-Sex.aspx

Foy, C. (2022, October 13). *Beauty standards, mental health, and their
eye-catching relationship.* FHE Health – Addiction & Mental Health
Care. https://fherehab.com/learning/beauty-standards-mental-health#:
~:text=Negative%20body%20image%20can%20lead

Gavin, M. (2018, February). *Why exercise is wise (for teens) - KidsHealth.*
Kidshealth.org. https://kidshealth.org/en/teens/exercise-wise.html

Gehman, W. (2021, February 25). *Teaching your teen to drive:
How to change a tire - car maintenance.* Strickler Insurance Agency
Inc. https://stricklerinsurance.com/blog/teaching-your-teen-to-drive-h
ow-to-change-a-tire/

*Gender identity, gender diversity and gender dysphoria: chil-
dren and teenagers.* (2021, March 15). Raising Children Network. https://raisingchildren.net.au/pre-teens/development/pre-teens-g
ender-diversity-and-gender-dysphoria/gender-identity

Gordon, S. (n.d.). *Everything your teen needs to know about setting
boundaries.* Verywell Family. Retrieved September 28, 2023, from
https://www.verywellfamily.com/boundaries-what-every-teen-needs-to-k
now-5119428#:~:text=Boundaries%20are%20limits%20teens%20establis
h

Health Direct. (2018, May 4). *Anxiety in teenagers.* Healthdirect.gov.au;
Healthdirect Australia. https://www.healthdirect.gov.au/anxiety-in-teen
agers

Healthwise Staff. (2022, August 2). *Normal menstrual cycle in teens: Care instructions*. Myhealth.alberta.ca. https://myhealth.alberta.ca/Health/aftercareinformation/pages/conditio ns.aspx?hwid=av2813#:~:text=The%20menstrual%20cycle%20is%20the

Hearn, P. (2022, September 12). *The 7 best sites with lists of jobs for teenagers*. Online Tech Tips. https://www.online-tech-tips.com/cool-we bsites/the-7-best-sites-with-lists-of-jobs-for-teenagers/

Hebert, M. (n.d.). *Creating a career vision board: A visual guide to your dream career*. TopResume. Retrieved October 21, 2023, from https://www.topresume.com/career-advice/creating-a-career-vision-boar d-a-visual-guide-to-your-dream-career#:~:text=You%20can%20find%20i mages%20and

Heger, E. (2022, May 19). *The sneaky ways social media can sabotage your body image — and 3 easy tips to help you break the cycle*. Insider. https://www.insider.com/guides/health/mental-health/how-socia l-media-affects-body-image

Helping Your Teen Through an Unhealthy Relationship. (2019, April 30). Womenshealth.gov. https://www.womenshealth.gov/blog/unhealthy-te en-relationships

Hideout, H. (2020, February 7). *Teach teens how to meal plan like a pro*. Homeschool Hideout. https://homeschoolhideout.com/teach-teens-ho w-to-meal-plan/

Hoshaw, C. (2021, February 26). *Body awareness: How to deepen your connection with your body*. Healthline. https://www.healthline.com/hea lth/mind-body/body-awareness#physical-exercises

How to Spot Signs of a Toxic Teen Relationship - Troubled Teens. (2022, February 23). TroubledTeens.com. https://troubledteens.com/troubled -teen-blog/toxic-teen-relationships/

Hrynkow, J. (2023). *How do you foster a positive and supportive family environment?* www.linkedin.com . https://www.linkedin.com/advice/0/how-do-you-foster-positive-supp ortive-family#:~:text=Try%20to%20set%20aside%20some

Indeed Editorial Team. (n.d.). *How to research career paths in 8 steps (with benefits).* Indeed Career Guide. https://www.indeed.com/career-advice/f inding-a-job/how-to-research-career

John Hopkins Medicine. (2019). *The growing child: Adolescent 13 to 18 years.* John Hopkins Medicine. https://www.hopkinsmedicine.org/healt h/wellness-and-prevention/the-growing-child-adolescent-13-to-18-years

Kirsten. (2018, March 26). *7 Things to expect from your first bra fitting.* Inner Secrets Lingerie. https://www.innersecrets.co.za/7-things-to-expec t-from-your-first-bra-fitting/

Lai, S. (2022, February 24). *How do we solve social media's eating disorder problem?* Brookings. https://www.brookings.edu/articles/how-do-we-so lve-social-medias-eating-disorder-problem/

Lang, D., Cone, N., Jones, T., Learning, L., College, O., Lally, M., & Valentine-French, S. (2022). Physical Development in Adolescence. *I a s t a t e . p r e s s b o o k s . p u b .* https://iastate.pressbooks.pub/individualfamilydevelopment/chapter/ph ysical-development-in-adolescence/#:~:text=These%20changes%20inclu de%20a%20growth

Lindsay, J. (2022, March 4). *What do girls need from their mentors?* ww w.linkedin.com. https://www.linkedin.com/pulse/what-do-girls-need-fr om-mentors-joy-lindsay

Lyness, D. (2018). *How can I improve my self-esteem? (for teens) - Kid-sHealth.* Kidshealth.org. https://kidshealth.org/en/teens/self-esteem.ht ml

Makvana, H. (2019, March 26). *69 Interest-ing and fun hobbies for teenagers.* MomJunc-tion. https://www.momjunction.com/articles/teenagers-hobbies_0047 4362/#:~:text=Engaging%20in%20hobbies%20can%20support

Marrocco, J., & McEwen, B. (2016). Sex in the brain: hormones and sex differences. *Sex Differences, 18*(4), 373–383. https://doi.org/10.31887/d cns.2016.18.4/jmarrocco

Monroe, H. (2018). *The importance of sleep for teen mental health.* US News & World Report; U.S. News & World Re-port. https://health.usnews.com/health-care/for-better/articles/2018-0

7-02/the-importance-of-sleep-for-teen-mental-health

Morin, LCSW, A. (n.d.). *How to foster stronger bonds between your kids.* Verywell Family. https://www.verywellfamily.com/how-to-create-strong er-bonds-among-siblings-4778201

NiDirect. (2015, December 2). *Healthy eating for adolescents | nidirect.* w ww.nidirect.gov.uk. https://www.nidirect.gov.uk/articles/healthy-eating -adolescents#:~:text=The%20teenage%20years%20are%20a

Patchin, J. W. (2017, December 4). *Teens talk: What works to stop cyber-bullying - cyberbullying research center.* Cyberbullying Research Center. https://cyberbullying.org/teens-talk-works-stop-cyberbullying

Patwal, S. (2014, December 12). *Personal hygiene for teens: Importance and tips   to   teach   them.* MomJunction. https://www.momjunction.com/articles/hygiene-tips-for-your-teens_00 116170/#:~:text=Teenagers%20must%20maintain%20proper%20hygien e

Prinsloo, E. (2022, February 3). *Why self-esteem is important to your mental   health.* Life   Path   Health. https://www.lifepathgroup.co.za/why-self-esteem-is-important-to-your -mental-health/#:~:text=People%20with%20healthy%20self%2Desteem

Puberty basics (for teens) - Nemours KidsHealth. (n.d.). Kidshealth.org . https://kidshealth.org/en/teens/puberty.html#:~:text=Hormones%20f rom%20the%20brain%20trigger

Rahman, LCSW, I. (2022, August 26). *How to leave a toxic relation-ship.* https://www.choosingtherapy.com/how-to-leave-a-toxic-relationsh ip/#:~:text=Practice%20self%2Dcare%20by%20surrounding

Raising Children Network. (2017, December 11). *Physical changes in puberty: girls and boys.* Raising Children Net-work. https://raisingchildren.net.au/pre-teens/development/puberty-se xual-development/physical-changes-in-puberty

Raypole, C. (2022, February 28). *How many thoughts do you have per day? And other FAQs.* Healthline. https://www.healthline.com/health/h ow-many-thoughts-per-day

Rodgers, R. (2020). *Media and body image in children and adolescents |*

Education in the digital age : Healthy and happy children | OECD iLibrary. www.oecd-Ilibrary.org. https://www.oecd-ilibrary.org/sites/9d2ea b3d-en/index.html?itemId=/content/component/9d2eab3d-en

Rutledge, P. (2022, February 3). *Online dating and teens: Looking for love in digital places*. Www.linkedin.com. https://www.linkedin.com/pulse/o nline-dating-teens-looking-love-digital-places-rutledge-phd-mba/

Sally. (2021, June 7). *The best healthy lunches for teens: 30+ ideas they'll love*. Real Mom Nutrition. https://www.realmomnutrition.com/healthy-lun ch-ideas-for-teens/

Santos, E., & Noggle, C. A. (2011). *Synaptic pruning* (S. Goldstein & J. A. Naglieri, Eds.). Springer Link; Springer US. https://link.springer.com/10.1007%2F978-0-387-79061-9_2856#: ~:text=Synaptic%20pruning%20refers%20to%20the

sbrands. (2021, January 31). *The importance of creating a study schedule and sticking to it*. Student Brands. https://studentbrands.co.za/career-guidance/the-importance-of-creating -a-study-schedule-and-sticking-to-it/#:~:text=Tips%20to%20Stick%20to %20Your%20Study%20Schedule&text=Calculate%20the%20time%20yo u%20need

Shah, K. (2014). *10 Common teenage problems and solutions | teenage social problems*. JBCN International School. https://www.jbcnschool.edu.in/b log/common-teenage-problems-solutions/

Sharkey, S. (2022, May 3). *Financial literacy for teenagers: Key money tips for teens*. Clever Girl Finance. https://www.clevergirlfinance.com/financial-literacy-for-teenage rs/#:~:text=Financial%20literacy%20for%20teenagers%20starts

Smith, J. (2021, June 12). *Basic household maintenance tasks for teenagers*. Engineering America. https://www.engamerica.com/basic-household-re pairs-for-teens/

Smith, K. (2020, November 24). *6 Common triggers of teen stress*. Psyco m.net - Mental Health Treatment Resource since 1996. https://www.ps ycom.net/common-triggers-teen-stress

Solstice East. (2019, July 10). *The effect of social media on body image in*

teen girls. Solstice East. https://solsticeeast.com/blog/the-effect-of-social
-media-on-body-image-in-teen-girls/

Speaking of psychology: Anxiety and teen girls, with Lisa Damour, PhD.
(2022). Apa.org. https://www.apa.org/news/podcasts/speaking-of-psyc
hology/anxiety-teen-girls

Spinks, S. (2000, March 9). *Work in progress - Adolescent brains are a work
in progress | inside the teenage brain | FRONTLINE | PBS.* www.pbs.org.
https://www.pbs.org/wgbh/pages/frontline/shows/teenbrain/work/adol
escent.html#:~:text=Changes%20in%20the%20Prefrontal%20Cortex&te
xt=As%20the%20prefrontal%20cortex%20matures

Spring, G. (2022, April 28). *5 Common issues that teen girls face.* Girl
Spring. https://www.girlspring.com/5-common-issues-that-teen-girls-fa
ce/

Spring, G. (2023, February 7). *A guide for teen girls with
anxiety: How to make mindfulness a part of your life.* Girl
Spring. https://www.girlspring.com/a-guide-for-teen-girls-with-anxiety
-how-to-make-mindfulness-a-part-of-your-life/

Stephenson, T. (2023, May 1). *Teen growing pains and self-identity.*
Monash   Lens.
https://lens.monash.edu/@education/2023/05/01/1385697/building-a
-powerful-self-identity-why-it-matters-for-adolescents#:~:text=Encourag
e%20self%2Dreflection%3A%20Adolescents%20need

Stinger, C. (2021, September 26). *10 Unspoken cooking tips every teen
should know.* The Teen Magazine. https://www.theteenmagazine.com/1
0-unspoken-cooking-tips-every-teen-should-know

Sweet, J. (2021, June 8). *Attentive listening helps teens share their
challenges,   study   finds.*   Verywell   Mind.
https://www.verywellmind.com/attentive-listening-helps-teens-share-the
i   r   -   c   h   a   l   l   e   n   g   e   s
5189401#:~:text=%E2%80%9CTeens%20are%20very%20self%2Daware

*Talking   to   Your   Parents   or   Other   Adults   (for
Teens)   -   Nemours   KidsHealth.*   (n.d.).   Kidshealth.org
. https://kidshealth.org/en/teens/talk-to-parents.html#:~:text=Talk%20
About%20Everyday%20Stuff%20%E2%80%94%20and

Techniques and Tips for Listening and Note Taking. (n.d.). www.student .unsw.edu.au. https://www.student.unsw.edu.au/notetaking-tips

Teenage Hormones & Sexuality. (2012, December 15). Newport Academy. https://www.newportacademy.com/resources/empowering-teens/teenag e-hormones-and-sexuality/#:~:text=Teen%20hormones%20affect%20tee nagers

Teens, R. H. (2019, December 31). *Tips to help your teen cultivate their passion | alcohol & drug education for parents of OC teens.* Raising Healthy Teens. https://raisinghealthyteens.org/tips-to-help-your-teen-cultivate-t heir-passion/

The five most flattering dresses for your body shapes. (2016, May 7). www .loveyourdress.ca. https://www.loveyourdress.ca/dress-blog/the-most-fla ttering-dresses-for-your-body-shape/

Ultimate guide: Copper's guide to budgeting (for teens). (n.d.). www.getco pper.com. https://www.getcopper.com/guide/budgeting

Using Effective Time Management To Improve Your Studying. (2019). Educationcorner.com. https://www.educationcorner.com/effective-tim e-management.html

Vo, Dr. D. (n.d.). *Guided meditations.* www.mindfulnessforteens.com. https://www.mindfulnessforteens.com/guided-meditations

Williams, G. (2019, March 25). *6 Apps teens can use to manage mon-ey.* HuffPost. https://www.huffpost.com/entry/money-apps-for-teens-a nd-parents_l_5c979128e4b01ebeef108c34

youth.GOV. (2022). *LGBT | Youth.gov.* Youth.gov. https://youth.gov/yo uth-topics/lgbt

Zander, I. van der. (2012, March 20). *Teen consent and boundary skills.* Kidpower International. https://www.kidpower.org/library/article/teen -boundaries/

Made in the USA
Monee, IL
18 July 2024

61899112R10079